Countrywomen

Countrywomen

by Emma Ford

BXTREE

First published in Great Britain in 1994 by
Boxtree Limited

Based on the series *Countrywomen* made by John Peel Productions,
from an original idea by Paddy McCreanor.
Text © Emma Ford 1994
Photographs © Nick Wood 1994
(with the exception of the following plate section photographs: page 1 –
middle and bottom © Dawn Warr; page 2 – *right bottom*, page 3 – *middle
and bottom* © Judy Bowser; page 4 – *bottom left and right* © Mother Mary
Agnes; page 5 – *bottom left and right* © Lynn Woodward; page 6 – *top* ©
Katy Cropper, *bottom* © Lancashire Evening Telegraph; page 7 – *bottom*
© Jean Lomas; page 8 – *bottom right* © Keystone Press Agency
Line illustrations © Antony Rhodes

The right of Emma Ford to be identified as Author of this
Work has been asserted by her in accordance with the
Copyright, Designs and Patents Act 1988

1 3 5 7 9 10 8 6 4 2

Designed by Behram Kapadia
Typeset by SX Composing, Essex, England
Printed and bound in Finland by WSOY, Juva for

Boxtree Limited
Broadwall House
21 Broadwall
London SE1 9PL

A CIP catalogue entry for this book is available from the
British Library

ISBN 1 85283 916 3

Front jacket and back flap photograph by Nick Wood.
Back jacket photographs (top three) by Nick Wood.
Bottom three photographs courtesy of Lynn Woodward,
Katy Cropper and Mother Mary Agnes.

(*Every effort has been made to trace all copyright holders for this book. In the
event that any omissions have been made, the publishers apologise and will be glad
to make proper acknowledgements in future editions of this publication.*)

Contents

Acknowledgements

Firstly, I would like to thank Paddy McCreanor for including me in the *Countrywomen* series and for his faith and perseverence in turning this book from an idea into a reality. Secondly, I must thank Judy and David Bowser, Mother Mary Agnes and Sister Mary Clare, Dawn Warr and her parents, Lynn Woodward and her parents, and Katy Cropper, all of whom found time for me in their busy schedules to outline the chapters and to check them for accuracy. I must also thank Patrick Walsh, Antony Rhodes for his line drawings, Nick Wood for his wonderful photographs, Fraser Hannah for his help and enthusiasm and Boxtree for telescoping their publication schedule to the minimum. Finally, I must add that I am humbly grateful to my husband, Steve, for undertaking the shopping and cooking on top of his other chores, while I wrote.

Preface

I greatly enjoyed researching this book as it gave me the opportunity to meet some remarkable women. Whilst our lives and careers are very different, I found that we have a lot in common. Primarily, we are extremely determined – I think our friends, colleagues and families might even say stubbon – and it is this determination which has driven us forward to achieve our aims, regardless of the setbacks we have encountered *en route*.

Despite the fact that we have succeeded in male-dominated roles, I did not find one amongst the women featured here who classed herself as a feminist. We have all merely got on and done our thing, with such single-mindedness that we have never stopped to consider issues such as equality. Frequently, our lives have been tough. Often we have found ourselves outside in filthy weather, doing heavy, dirty tasks, which have left us with little time or energy to concentrate on more feminine pursuits. To date, only Judy has found the time to have children.

In compensation, we have the countryside. We are all happier outdoors than in. We share a love of animals – domesticated and wild. We relish daily the peace and beauty of our rural surroundings and feast our eyes on the abundant wildlife. In our roles as countrywomen, our lives have been daubed liberally with the rich colours of nature. We are enormously privileged.

CHAPTER 1

Judy Bowser

ESTATE OWNER/STALKER

O n her sixtieth birthday, Judy Bowser climbed to the top of Ben Mor – at 3842 feet, the highest peak on her property – and surveyed the land which had been hers since her twenty-first birthday. Gazing down on the surrounding hills and glens, her thoughts were filled not with her achievement, but with a sense of security, as she reflected for the umpteenth time that whatever struggles the human custodians of the estate had suffered and would suffer to keep it viable, the mountains would still be there, unchanged, a thousand years hence.

Judy was lucky to have been born. A month prior to her birth, her mother overturned the car she was driving. It rolled down a small bank and both mother and baby were fortunate to survive. However, perhaps showing some of the determination which has subsequently coloured her life, Judy popped out on time on 21 July 1925, apparently unscathed.

Judy's family have been connected with Auchlyne Estate since 1888. At that time her great grandfather, John Millar Crabbie, made some money from the whisky business and decided that he would like to rent a grouse moor. Auchlyne, which belonged to the Marquis of

Breadalbane who owned a great deal of land in the area, came up for rent. The grouse shooting on Auchlyne was excellent in those days and suited John Crabbie's purpose admirably. After his death in 1898, his son, Judy's grandfather, continued to take the sporting rights on the estate. In 1905, he changed the family name to Crabbe, after being blackballed from the New Club in Edinburgh for 'being in the trade'. Judy's grandfather died the year she was born, but her father, John Gordon Crabbe, maintained the family's sporting rights, and the family tradition of spending the summers at Auchlyne.

Judy's childhood was spent at Duncow, the family estate, five miles west of Dumfries. She had one older brother, Peter, and a younger sister, Edwina. Her older sister had died in infancy. It was at Duncow that Judy learned to enjoy country life and country pursuits. Escaping each day from the clutches of their governess, the children would scatter across the estate hell-bent on disrupting its wildlife. Edwina showed much less interest in country pursuits than Judy, who rapidly developed into a tomboy, following her older brother as the two of them learned to fish in the muddy ponds that were dotted across the estate.

The children were never without animals. One of their more unusual waifs and strays was an orphaned red deer hind called Sylvia. Initially, Sylvia was a great success. She would follow the children around, grazing or sun-bathing on the lawn through the long summer days, and generally getting on well with everyone, including the dogs. However, like the vast majority of hand-reared non-domesticated animals, she became a problem as she grew bigger. To seek attention, she developed the habit of rearing up at the children and lashing out with her hooves. Judy's father made the unpopular decision that she would have to go, and go she did, to the Linlithgo family at Hopetoun House, a large stately home on the outskirts of Edinburgh. Hopetoun had a herd of park deer, with whom, it was hoped, Sylvia would integrate. The deer were kept in the park by a perimeter fence, but they did not have to be fenced away from the house, as, born and bred in the park, they stayed in their own territory, giving humans a wide berth.

Sylvia had no such scruples. She missed her young friends back at Duncow and moped around the outside of the house, eating the gardens and mugging visitors. The final straw came when she climbed the steps to the front door and discovered that someone had failed to shut it properly. Pushing her way in, she was delighted to find a large bowl of flowers, which had been thoughtfully placed on the hall table. These she demolished swiftly before continuing on her voyage of destruction through the downstairs rooms. In every room she discovered a variety of gourmet snacks in the form of plants and cut flowers, all of which she devoured with relish. When she was finally discovered, she was ejected unceremoniously and sent post haste to Edinburgh Zoo, where she lived to a ripe old age.

The summer was the favourite time of year, for in August the family would migrate north to Auchlyne for the start of the grouse season. A convoy of cars and the coalman's lorry were employed to shift the family and all its household and sporting paraphernalia on the 126-mile journey up to Auchlyne. Judy, feverishly excited by the prospect of spending two months roaming the countryside at will, would travel in the car with her father and was usually sick during the journey. Her earliest memory of being at Auchlyne was in the summer of 1928, when she had whooping cough and much to her fury, was confined to the top floor of the house. Everybody else was enjoying themselves outside and the monotony was relieved only by brief visits from the family cat, but even this made itself scarce after Judy managed to be violently sick over it one morning. Despite being vigorously washed and scrubbed, the unfortunate animal was still matted and eventually its fur had to be trimmed with a small pair of scissors.

Judy's later memories of Auchlyne are somewhat happier. The Crabbe children were pretty much allowed to run wild for the summer, coming back into the family fold for various highlights such as the Killin show, which was held annually in the park at Lord Breadalbane's home. One of the main attractions of the show was the pipe band, which opened the show by marching up the park in full ceremonial dress. When she was about six, Judy decided that she would like to take her own tiny set of bagpipes, which someone had been unwise enough to give her, and march with the band. Lurking in the wings she shot purposefully in amongst the pipers before anyone could stop her and completed the march, mercifully without managing to get a peep out of her diminutive bagpipes.

When Judy was big enough, she was allowed to join the flankers for some of the grouse drives. The first time she completed two drives, Judy was paid five shillings. With a keen sense of purpose, she managed to save a further 2s 6d and promptly bought an air gun in the local paper shop in Killin. New horizons opened up. One of the keepers had two young sons, who aided and abetted Judy as, with malice aforethought, she stalked the local wildlife with dogged determination and escalating ability. She was a naturally bloodthirsty child, and pretty much everything that moved got it, from rabbits to blackbirds. Even the pike in the pond were unable to bask in the long summer evenings in peace, as with scant disregard for the laws of refraction, Judy took pot shots at them from the bank. She discovered that she couldn't kill them with the shot, but was delighted to find that it shook them up so badly that they would be quite stunned and would float on their backs to the surface. If she was quick enough, she could then flip them out by the tail, before they recovered their senses and swam off.

Around this time, Judy also managed to persuade her parents to buy her a ferret. She christened it Brumble, and it proved to be a great bonus. Now the rabbits came under assault underground, as well as on the surface. Judy could either use Brumble to flush the rabbits into nets pegged around their holes, or allow them to bolt across open ground, thus enabling her to sharpen her skills with the gun.

Judy progressed from an airgun to a twenty-bore shotgun and aged twelve or thirteen, she would head off with it in the morning, through the woods at the back of the house, returning only when her game bag was full to bursting. Rather than risk incurring the wrath of the keeper, she would dutifully paunch and dress her kills before hanging them in the game larder – a discipline to which she still adheres. By the age of fourteen, her prowess as a shot was such that she was permitted to join the shooting parties in her own right.

The highlight of Judy's early shooting days came when she shot her first stag at the age of twelve. On her return home, a member of the family asked if she was surprised when the stag fell and she replied, 'No, not really – it was bigger than the sparrows I shoot with my air gun and as I hit it in the right place, it was bound to fall.' This was the start of a lifelong passion for stalking which Judy has subsequently passed down to her daughter Emma. During the same year, Judy's father had the opportunity to buy Auchlyne from the Breadalbane family. He managed to acquire the house, four farms and ten thousand acres of land for ten thousand pounds. The family's association with the estate was thereby secured.

In her early teens, Judy began to show a keen interest in gardening. This puzzled her parents somewhat, as it was a bloodless pursuit and her enthusiasm for it was therefore quite out of character. Every day she would disappear into the depths of the garden with the old gardener, apparently keen to help him with whatever he was up to at the time. Intrigued, Judy's father followed her one morning and was intensely annoyed to see wisps of cigarette smoke emerging from Judy's general direction. Sagely, he threatened to take her gun away if he saw her smoking again. Judy merely ensured that he didn't catch her a second time.

Back at Duncow in the winter, the shooting continued as, much to Judy's delight, her father leased some good duck shooting on the river Nith. Jock Crabbe, as well as being an excellent shot, was a first-class horseman and bought Judy her first pony, Polly. Judy was uncharacteristically nervous of Polly and of her subsequent ponies. This was largely because of her experiences in the hunting field. Encouraged to hunt with the Dumfriesshire pack, she found she could never stop her mounts, which carted her in true Thelwellian style in the wake of her father's hunter. 'Come along, Judy!' her father would cry, pitching his mount straight over the edge of a terrifyingly steep drop and Judy would have little choice but to follow, clinging on for grim death. This was a rapid and somewhat unwelcome progression from her early efforts to master riding, when she would potter around in a basket on the back of Nellie, the donkey at Auchlyne.

The farming at Duncow never amounted to very much. The thousand acres or so was devoted to tenanted arable and woodland and was exceedingly stony, so Judy learned very little about farming during her childhood and teenage years. The family did, however, keep a couple of dozen hens and two house cows, for milk and for butter which was produced in their own dairy. Whilst she was at Auchlyne one summer, Judy persuaded the maid on the farm next door to teach her how to milk – an experience which was to stand her in good stead in the years to come.

It came as a huge blow when Judy's mother decided to send her to boarding school in the south at the age of thirteen. Southover Manor was situated in the Sussex town of Lewes and was Judy's idea of purgatory. The front door opened on to Southover high street and the rear on to a dreary little games field which backed on to the railway line to Brighton. Her life there was in such stark contrast to the freedom which she had enjoyed in Scotland that Judy felt as though she was in prison – a state of mind which was reflected in her academic achievement, as she was regularly bottom of the class bar one. Every time she received a letter from her mother, she would burst into tears.

The Second World War came to her rescue. After Dunkirk, her mother decided that it would be safer for Judy to return to Scotland. Judy was thrilled to receive this news, firmly believing that it would mean no more school that term. Her mother, however, had different ideas and within two days of arriving back at Duncow, Judy found herself enrolled at Gargunnock House, near Stirling.

Despite Judy's fears, Gargunnock proved to be a considerable improvement on the wretched Southover Manor. It was, to all intents and purposes, a finishing school, which had been evacuated from France for the duration of the War. The curriculum was a joy to behold and included such jollies as skating at Falkirk ice rink on Wednesday afternoons, as well as more typical finishing school subjects, such as flower arranging, history of art and music lessons. To Judy it was comparative bliss and she even managed to settle down academically, passing 'O' level English and French. She also discovered music during her time at Gargunnock and took up various instruments. The only drawback was that her tutors wanted her to play Mozart and Beethoven, while she much preferred to play more popular tunes, which she cajoled out of instruments ranging from a swanee whistle to an accordion, with little ability but great enthusiasm.

After Gargunnock, Judy went to Shamley Green – a cookery school. Here she was taught to do laundry, fold napkins and lay the table as well as various culinary skills. This she considered to be money well spent, firstly as she enjoyed it and secondly as her parents' household, which had consisted of ten staff before the war, had dwindled to two post-war and the family was forced to come to terms with the fact that if they wanted something done on the domestic front, they would have to learn how to do it themselves.

At the age of eighteen, Judy completed her time at Shamley Green. With the war still on, young girls were not allowed to sit around at home, so Judy was in the position of having to explore her options. She decided that the Wrens were more upmarket than the ATS, so she applied, but was told that the only posts available were for cooks or stewards. She didn't think that was for her, so being an outdoor girl, she plumped for the land army. This was a good move, as it provided Judy with the opportunity to learn the farming skills which, as it turned out, she was going to need in the future. It also gave her the chance to learn to work with people and to develop the discipline necessary to complete long hours of heavy labour. Judy headed south to a cousin's farm in Wiltshire and was soon working a seventy-two-hour week for £3 10s, half of which she promptly had to hand over for her keep.

Judy's tasks included milking, cooking, looking after the children and a plethora of other jobs associated with working on a mixed farm during the war. She also had a horse and cart with which to do the milk round for the local village. Although it was extremely hard work, Judy found it interesting and enjoyable. Her mother wrote frequently, giving her news of the rest of the family. At the time, her father was serving with the Lothian and Border Yeomanry, but he was not overseas, so the family had no need to worry about him unduly. Sadly, however, Judy's brother Peter was killed in action in France in 1944.

In one particular letter, Judy's mother wrote 'Suie is on the market. I wonder who the silly ass will be who will buy Suie.' Suie was an estate of approximately eleven thousand acres which lay across the other side of the glen from Auchlyne. As she pondered this news, a postscript at the bottom of the letter caught Judy's attention. It read 'Your father has bought Suie.' The farming implications of the extra ground were largely irrelevant to Judy's father. He wanted it in order to have sufficient shooting on his own ground for all his friends, who came to Auchlyne for a full week of grouse shooting during the season.

Judy's social life whilst she was in the land army was not particularly exciting. With a five a.m. start and a six p.m. finish, seven days a week, she didn't have a huge amount of energy for making whoopee in the evenings. However, when she did have the stamina, Judy would climb on to her bicycle and pedal off into Malmsbury and Cirencester, where she would spend the evening fending off GIs who wanted to walk her home. She was not, to their disappointment, very interested in acquiring a boyfriend as she was more interested in the work she was doing. Indeed, one of her more memorable evenings was spent on a bale of straw in Reading market, in the company of a dairy shorthorn bull, which was to be sold the following day.

Judy had never been taught how to drive, although when she was thirteen, she and the two keeper's sons, over whom she had exerted an extremely naughty influence, would drive the cars belonging to guests at Auchlyne in and out of the garages, while their owners were out shooting. Armed with this early experience, Judy had no compunction about agreeing to take a car from the farm half a mile up the road to the garage, when requested to do so one day by her cousin, who had no idea that she couldn't drive. Heading off in a reasonably straight line, she ground her way cheerfully through the gears and managed to get the little car into third before reaching the garage.

At this time, there were three Italian prisoners working on the farm. Periodically, they were allowed to go back to their former camp to visit their chums. One Sunday evening, Judy's cousin asked her to go and pick up the prisoners. After an exciting journey over to the camp, Judy pulled up outside, and out came the prisoners. They, however, knew perfectly well that Judy had never been taught to drive and seeing her behind the wheel, they shot back inside like scalded cats. Fearing that she would never be allowed to drive the car again if she returned home without them, Judy turned on her full powers of persuasion and eventually succeeded in getting them to climb miserably into the back seat, before completing a somewhat erratic journey back to the farm. Unknown to Judy's mother, the prisoners slept in the room next door to Judy and there was no lock on their door! Judy – blithely unselfconscious – never gave this fact a second thought.

After two years in the land army, Judy returned home to Duncow and worked in the gardens until the end of the war. This she enjoyed and felt to be good experience. During this period, her father asked her which of the family's two estates she would like to inherit – with the death of Peter in the war, she was now the eldest and in the absence of another son, she could have her choice between Duncow or Auchlyne and Suie. For Judy the choice was obvious and the decision was made that on her twenty-first birthday she would inherit Auchlyne.

In the spring and summer of her twenty-first year, Judy ran wild at Auchlyne. She stayed at the local hotel and filled her days burning heather, clipping sheep and generally entering into whatever was going on. She managed to catch her first salmon and the sporting season progressed much as usual, with grouse shooting and the stags, before she returned to Duncow for hunting in the winter. The sheer pleasure of knowing that the estate she had loved since childhood was now hers was coupled joyfully with the knowledge that, at last, nobody could tell her what to do.

The period immediately surrounding Judy's twenty-first birthday in 1946 was notable for several other reasons, one of which was that she got her first car as a present from her parents. It was a Triumph Roadster, in metallic silver, with blue leather upholstery, a drophead and a dickey at the back with two little seats. It was very smart and Judy was frightfully pleased with it, although she was slightly disappointed that it would do a maximum of only 70 m.p.h.

More importantly, it was also during this period that she met David Bowser. She left Duncow one morning to travel to Ecclefechan, to pick up an autobike (a heavy pedal bike with small engine) which an aunt was giving her for her birthday. Her mother had disappeared in the Bentley to go to the dentist in Edinburgh. When Judy returned, she saw that a Bentley was parked outside the house and she was curious as to how her mother had managed to get back from Edinburgh so quickly. However, a closer inspection of the Bentley revealed a different number plate and solid wheels, as opposed to the spoked wheels of her mother's car. Approaching across the lawn was a small group of people, one of whom Judy recognized as a neighbour, Walter Duncan, who owned the ground just across the wall from one of the ponds where Judy used to fish. The other three were introduced as Walter's cousins, the Bowsers, and their son David. Apparently, they had gathered for a family wedding and had just popped over to say hello. The discussion led to what they were going to do that evening and the long and the short of it was that Judy was invited to accompany them to the pictures. David, it transpired, was in the Scots Guards and although he was only twenty at the time, his parents allowed him to drive the party in the Bentley that evening. Keen to impress Judy, he changed gear far more often than was necessary, just to prove that he could do it.

David Bowser clearly realized quite early on that Judy was not the type of girl who would be particularly interested in joining a glitzy social set for evenings on the town. For their first date in London, therefore, he went on a recce to the Dairy Show, to see if he felt this would interest her. Interest her it did and she travelled down to London to meet him and to go to the show. Things progressed after this and when David went to Cambridge, Judy accepted a steady stream of invitations for May Balls and the Queen Charlotte's Ball, as she generally made an effort to fit in, albeit without much relish, with the accepted pattern of social events. Aside from this, they had much in common — David also enjoyed shooting and fishing and consequently when, in 1950, David proposed on the Dochart river bank, Judy accepted.

They spent the first eight years of their marriage at Auchlyne. During Judy's first two summers after inheriting Auchlyne, she had stayed in the nearby hotel, as there was no household in the main house, but during her third summer, she had stayed in the house on her own and had continued to stay there during the summers that followed. The house was therefore habitable, but without central heating, as the family had not been in the habit of spending the winter there. It was bitterly cold. Judy and David had a stove in the smoking room – an addition to the house which Judy's grandfather had built on – and in there they could get quite cosy in the evenings, but the rest of the house and the bedrooms in particular, resembled Siberia. However, delighted at last to be living at the place she loved, Judy was undaunted and threw herself into running the farm, the sporting side of the estates and the household. Compared to the pre-war days, she had a tiny household – a housekeeper who cooked and a keeper's wife who cleaned.

In 1952, Judy went back to Dumfries, to her mother and the local maternity hospital to give birth to Emma. In the ensuing years, she returned twice more, every other year, to have Niall and Susan. Typically, Judy was not a great believer in taking things easy during pregnancy. She was supposed to be pigeon shooting on the day Niall was born, but mercifully she decided in the morning that she didn't really feel like it and later was rushed to the maternity hospital. Tiring of this bi-annual interruption to her normal schedule, Judy decided to have her fourth child, Fiona, at Auchlyne.

Unobligingly, Fiona refused to put in an appearance after nine months. Judy's life continued as normal while she waited impatiently for the baby's arrival. Late in the ninth month, she received a phone call from one of her tenant farmers, moaning about the stags which were coming off the high ground and eating his crops. Judy told him that the next time he saw them in his fields, he should phone her immediately.

At 3.45 the next morning, the phone rang. 'The stags are in m' fields,' Judy was informed, unceremoniously. Bulging with Fiona, Judy got her rifle and in the cold grey light of dawn she went next door and shot five of them. Then she returned home, so irritated by her condition that she swallowed a complete bottle of castor oil in an effort to dislodge Fiona. It was to no avail.

After a full ten months, Fiona was born on the drawing-room floor at Auchlyne. This, Judy deemed to be a sensible location, as she needed to give birth close to the only bathroom in the house and also close to the telephone. Judy finally managed to expel Fiona and out she popped, with the aid of the midwife and the local GP. Peering at the baby in the midwife's arms, Judy was horrified to see that it was a sickly blue colour and didn't look as though it was alive. It transpired that the cord was caught around Fiona's throat. The midwife was fortunately very experienced and cut the cord, put a tube down the baby's throat and slapped Fiona on the back. She promptly started to yell and the champagne was opened.

Judy and David's fifth child, Anna, was born at Argaty – David's family home near Stirling. David's parents, who had been living in Argaty, had built themselves another house on the estate and David, therefore, was expected to return home with his family to move into the main house. This they did in 1959. It came as a dreadful blow to Judy, who missed Auchlyne desperately. Argaty was an enormous house, with massive rooms, which as the central heating system was so old, never seemed to get really warm. For the children, it was a totally different prospect to Auchlyne. If they wanted to shoot, they couldn't just go, they had to ask the keeper and as a consequence, none of them were as keen on country pursuits as Judy would have liked. Judy lived for the summers, when, in mid July, they would head back to Auchlyne for the shooting season. By the end of August, a shadow would begin to fall across Judy, dulling her pleasure as she realized that fifty percent of their annual visit had passed. Before she knew it, they were down to their last week and then it was time to return to Argaty for the winter. As they left Auchlyne, she would cry until they rounded the bend at the end of the glen. Resigned, however, to this annual cycle, she cheered up quickly and began looking forward to next year.

The Bowser family spent twenty-five years at Argaty. During this time

Judy never knew if she would live at her beloved Auchlyne again. She visited it whenever she could but, inevitably, she lost touch with the intimate workings of the estate. Looking back on this period, Judy sees it as time lost – time when she could have been learning more about farming and improving her practical skills. It was a time when a great number of large estates began to come under pressure – the cost of labour was escalating and the big houses were tending to become comparatively run down, as landowners found themselves unable to afford the huge number of staff necessary to run them efficiently.

Argaty was no exception. It had become a drain on resources. Once the family had grown up and moved on, it was also a ludicrously large house for two people. David talked of moving into one of the farmhouses on the estate and finally he asked Niall if he wanted to live in Argaty. He decided it wouldn't be sensible – having seen the toll that maintaining Argaty House was taking on his father, he could not see how he could manage any better – so the decision was taken to sell the property.

Apart from stating categorically that she did not want to live in one of the farmhouses, Judy stayed quiet. She did not want to bring any additional pressure to bear on David at this time, but there was a chink of light at the end of her tunnel. Finally, as Argaty was about to be put on the market, she asked 'Where do we go now then?'

'We could go back to Auchlyne.' David told her.

'Oh, yes, we could.' Judy replied, trying her best to keep cool, so that he didn't realize how desperately she wanted to return.

'You'd have to put in central heating.'

'Oh, I think I could manage that.'

So in 1982 the family returned to live at Auchlyne. For Judy it was a marvellous relief. She put in central heating and set about taking on board the running of the business side of the estate and at long last she was able to devote herself to the seasonal pattern of work, related to the overall management of Auchlyne and Suie. Although this appeared to be something of a role reversal, David recognized both that Judy wanted to take over the day-to-day running of the estates and that she was capable of doing so. Moreover, the estates belonged to Judy, not to him, so he largely left her to it unless she needed his help. Nowadays, much of his time is taken up with good works and he holds an impressive list of titles relating to his work with the Church of Scotland and deer management. The former include the position of Chairman of the Property Committee of the Presbytery of Stirling. As such, he is responsible for the oversight of fifty ecclesiastical buildings. In his work relating to deer management, he was Chairman of the Scottish Deer Society 1989–1994 and he is still a member of the executive committee of Deer Management Groups. Despite holding these and a host of other positions, he still manages to find time to help Judy by doing the scheduling, paperwork and accounts relating to the estates' sporting lets and his daily responsibilities include shopping and collecting the papers.

Judy continues to run the farms, which have been gradually taken back in hand from tenants, as she has spearheaded the work to develop them to the stage where they can produce the income necessary to maintain the estates. Over the years, she has developed a great fondness for Highland cattle. Highland cattle come in all shades from black to white. The fold book at Auchlyne dates back to 1947 and looking back, Judy is particularly proud that she has personally managed the herd from the word go. She has always selected her cattle herself, rather than entrusting the task to a herd manager and now, after nearly fifty years, she has reached the top of the tree with her bloodlines, which are widely recognized as producing some of the finest Highland cattle in the world.

Judy gets very attached to her cattle – she can recognize all 200 or so bulls, cows, calves and heifers individually. The majority are Highlanders, but she also has a crossing herd. She spends a lot of time with her cattle, deriving great pleasure from being with them. Many of them know her too, and will come over to talk to her. She shows them, judges at shows, attends sales and reckons that the development of the herd is probably the major achievement in her life. She has won at the Highland Show and she has also won the championship there on three occasions. Curiously, doing well with the judges does not guarantee a high price for the beast in the sales – the champion bull failed to make a substantial sum when auctioned in the ring in 1981. Yet in 1994, Judy sold a bull which got nowhere in the judging for fourteen thousand guineas. It is partly this uncertainty which makes cattle sales so enjoyable for Judy, and she devotes a great deal of time and energy to getting cattle ready for the sales, which are her favourite event of the year.

Judy's year starts with the gathering of sheep. The breeding ewes need to come in from the hill – approximately two and a half thousand of them. It is a sociable time, as all the neighbours join in to help, with sheepdogs and as many able bodies as possible. When the neighbours are gathering their own sheep, they are helped in return. Everybody heads for the estate boundaries and the ewes are encouraged by the dogs and much whistling and shouting, to progress back across the hill to the pens on the farm. Here they are dipped, dosed and inoculated.

January is also the continuation of the hind stalking season, which finishes in the middle of February. A hind is a female red deer and the season for culling them runs from 21 October until 15 February. By definition, culling is the selective shooting of animals and birds which are liable otherwise to become too numerous – either to the detriment of their bloodline, or to the extent where the habitat cannot support their numbers. Most of the hind culling is done early in the season, before the harsh winter months cause them to lose condition. Part of Judy's initiative on the sporting front was to let the hind stalking to sporting clients. This income, which is in addition to the income for the venison, is beneficial to the estate and helps to subsidize costs.

February is the time for the Highland Cattle Society's Bull Sale. Four or five months prior to the sale, the work starts on bringing out the bulls and heifers selected for the sale. Apart from being an important business milestone in the year, it is also a social event for Judy, as she meets up with old friends and newcomers from all over the country and from abroad too. The judging is a time of tension and the bidding is extremely exciting, particularly if prices are high. At the end of each day, everyone gathers at the ceilidhs – noisy parties with Scottish dancing – to let off steam.

In February, too, the Cheviot ewes are scanned to see if they are in lamb. The scanner shows whether it will be a single lamb, or twins or triplets and this acts as a guideline for the feeding of the Cheviot flock which, being more valuable than the other breeds of sheep which Judy keeps, is fed supplementary food over the winter months.

If the weather is dry in March, Judy will try to do some heather burning, to help the grouse which feed on young heather shoots and to improve the grazing for the sheep and the deer. If the heather plants become too old and woody, they are no use as a source of food and thus old heather needs to be burned to generate new growth. Ideally approximately one tenth of the moor needs to be burned each year, so that the moor is being constantly recycled to produce good heather. Auchlyne averages ninety inches of rainfall a year, so some Springs it is too wet to get a fire going. Other years, when it is dry, it can be decidedly dodgy to light a fire, as in a good wind it can get out of control and burn too great an area. For this reason, Judy likes to supervise the burning personally, which she carries out together with the keeper, the stalker and her eldest daughter, Emma.

April heralds the lambing time – something about which Judy confesses to knowing very little and which the shepherds would apparently prefer that she stayed well away from. Judy's first attempt at lambing ended in her being unable to get the lamb out and having to shoot the ewe. Her next attempt was no more successful, as both the lamb and the ewe died. By this stage Judy had developed the reputation of being black-fingered with lambing. It was therefore with great trepidation that she risked interfering with another ewe. On her way down the field one day she saw the animal attempting to lamb. The head of the lamb was showing and it was greatly swollen – 'a chokey' as the shepherds term it. The ewe was in need of urgent assistance so, despite her abysmal track record, Judy rolled up her sleeves and, with a great heave, managed to pull the lamb out. She put it, blue and oedematous, under the exhausted mother's nose and disappeared quietly, hoping for the best. When she saw the shepherd, she told him what she had done – attempting to describe the ewe. As she spoke, a look of horror came over his face.

'That's my •••• ewe!' he spluttered. The shepherds are allowed to take a number of ewes as part of their remuneration.

'Oh Ian – I wouldn't have dared to catch it if I had known it was your ewe – I thought it was one of mine!'.

Clearly believing that if Judy had so much as looked at them, both ewe and lamb were bound to be dead, Ian rushed off to find them. Fortunately, he found them alive and well, but Judy is understandably disinclined to try her hand further at lambing, for although she would dearly love to be proficient at it, she recognizes it as one of many skills which she missed the opportunity to acquire during her years at Argaty.

The Highland cattle calve from 1 December. The pedigrees of all the calves are recorded in the herd book, together with their ancestors. The ideal time for a calf to be born is March or April, when the spring grass will improve the cows' milk. Unlike the lambing, Judy gets actively involved with the calving, pulling and heaving for a couple of hours sometimes to get the calf out. The heifers aren't mated until they are two years old, so it was with great alarm one spring that Judy discovered that one of her one-year-old Highland heifers was in calf. When the heifer tried to deliver it, she couldn't push it out – really she was no more than a calf herself – so the vet was called and he decided to do a caesarean section. Despite being game for any amount of hard and heavy work, Judy is decidedly squeamish when it comes to operations of any sort. However, her concern for the little heifer was such that she stayed to watch while the vet anaesthetized the heifer and opened her up. Fascinated, Judy watched with bated breath as he slid his hand inside and pulled out a tiny little calf, about the size of a cat. Incredibly, it was alive and watching it draw its first breath and snort, Judy was delighted that she had steeled herself to witness such a remarkable scene. For her, the Highlanders are part of the family and each new calf is cause for celebration.

In May, the keepers and Emma make a concerted effort on vermin control. They take terriers and visit all the dens on the hill, where the foxes live in holes and rocky outcrops. The terriers are sent down to bolt the fox and the keepers and Emma shoot them as they come out. This is essential work, as the foxes prey on young grouse and also on lambs, which they will frequently kill just for the hell of it. Judy gets really annoyed if she finds a lamb which has been killed by a fox purely out of devilment – maybe with only the tail or an ear chewed off. One morning some years ago, the shepherd reported to Judy that they had had eight lambs killed in a single night. This represented a considerable loss, so since this time, a great deal of leg work has been devoted to seeking out the hill-fox dens.

June is one of Judy's favourite months because it is the time when the clipping or shearing of the ewes takes place. Clipping is something that she really enjoys. The men use electric clippers, but Judy prefers to use hand shears, which are a lot slower, although she still manages to clip forty or fifty ewes in a day. It is a skill that she has been working to perfect for many years. As her back isn't as strong as it used to be, Judy prefers to sit down, rather than bend over, so she plants herself firmly on a V-shaped stool with four legs and arranges the sheep on its back, between her legs. She gets very hot and sticky with the exertion and ends the day black and blue with bruising, from the ewes' horns, when she traps their heads under her arm to hold them still.

'I think the staff probably think: "it's a pity she won't roll the wool or pack the wool, she'd get on better doing that than the clipping," but I don't pay any attention to that – I delegate the rolling of the wool and the packing of it to somebody else because I enjoy my clipping. I don't enjoy doing the wool and so they can think what they like about my efforts at the clipping, but I just do my own thing. Provided I give them a tot of whisky at the end, they don't say too much.'

The early summer is a good time to repair the miles of fencing on the estate. Good stock fences are essential, so Judy drives around in her little Renault van with a fencing kit in the back – spare posts, wire and tools. If, on her travels, she spies a stob which needs repairing or a broken wire, she hops out and repairs it herself. This she finds very satisfying, although when she settles in front of the television with her knitting in the evening, she often finds her hands are shaking from the exertion. In fact, Judy is generally quite handy and she likes buying tools and bits and pieces. She's a great believer in something for nothing and, like a magpie, if she sees anything lying in the road which could be used to repair a bit of machinery, she will stop and put it in her van. She claims that if she were suddenly to be given a vast sum of money, she would use it to put every inch of fencing on the estate in order and to paint and tidy the place so that it looked absolutely immaculate.

The Highland Show is one of the biggest events of Judy's year. It takes place in late June. Judy and her cattleman need to select the animals she is going to show six months in advance, which isn't particularly easy. The chosen animals are fed carefully for the intervening months, to build them up to their peak condition. Immediately prior to the show, their coats are groomed and groomed, until they fall silkily into place. Sadly, Highlanders are not looking their best in July, as they have lost their spectacular winter coat, which falls to a shining eight inches. However, everyone showing at the event is in the same boat and no beast is entered unless its owner believes that it has a good chance of winning a prize. The competition is therefore hot.

When a cow is led into the ring, Judy suffers from mixed emotions. She wants it to be placed first, but if it isn't, she is torn between wishing it had done better and relief that she doesn't have to go through the tension of watching it compete in the championship class, which is made up of the winners of each class. Judy, with legs shaking and a lump in her throat, had the distinction of watching a favourite cow win at the Highland Show two years running. To win at this level is a terrific accolade and an extremely good advertisement for the breeder.

After the tension of the Highland Show, Judy will frequently take a quiet walk up the hill to look for signs of grouse. If she flushes a young covey, or family group, she can often see if it has been a good breeding season by the number of young grouse which get up with the adult pair. She can also get an indication of how many grouse are around by following the sheep tracks – when the grouse are wet, they will come out on to the sheep tracks to dry off. By looking at the amount of grouse droppings on the tracks, Judy can assess the concentration of their numbers in that area. Grouse need grit to aid their digestion so, in July, sacks of grit are taken up on to the hill and distributed.

The early assessment of the grouse numbers is important, for although the family retains a couple of days of shooting, the majority is let to clients. If the grouse numbers look good, more days can be let and conversely, if it has been a poor breeding season, some of the let days may have to be cancelled. Judy still enjoys her shooting, but over the years she has mellowed and she is now much more friendly towards nature's flora and fauna than she was in her youth. This is in part due to the fact that there is now much less to shoot – certain species which were abundant in her childhood are now comparatively rare. One example is the blackcock or black grouse – a larger cousin of the red grouse. Blackgame, as they are called, used to be reasonably plentiful on Auchlyne and the guns would enjoy shooting these magnificent sporting birds. Now, however, Judy says: 'If a blackcock got up between my legs I wouldn't shoot it!' All the grouse shooting at Auchlyne and Suie is walked-up nowadays, with the guns ranging across the moor in a line, flushing the birds in their path as they walk. Sadly, there are no longer enough red grouse to accommodate the big driven days of Judy's childhood, when beaters would sweep the moor to drive the grouse in their hundreds, towards a line of guns.

The season for grouse shooting opens on the twelfth of August – the Glorious Twelfth, as it is known to those who look forward to this day. Following in the family tradition, the Bowser family gathers at Auchlyne a couple of days before the season opens. On the evening of the eleventh, there is an air of anticipation amongst the assembled company. Nobody knows what the next day will bring, but one thing is for certain – there will be a lot of walking and the less fit members of the party may well feel a twinge of trepidation.

At ten o'clock the next morning, the party sets off, complete with dogs and a picnic lunch. With any luck, the weather will be fine, with a light breeze blowing to cool the walkers. Hot, still days make for uncomfortable walking as the midges will appear and plague both human and canine members of the party. After a short walk uphill, the shooting party find themselves amongst the grouse. They walk in a line, with the dogs scenting a short distance ahead. When the grouse break from the cover of the heather, they streak away, hugging the contours of the ground. Walked-up grouse shooting is only for good shots, as it is widely considered to be one of the most difficult forms of shooting. Judy derives satisfaction from the fact that the entire party is made up of family – herself and David, Emma and three son-in-laws, together with Richard, Judy's grandson. After a strenuous morning, they rest on the hill for an hour at lunchtime, flaking out gratefully in the purple heather. One of the great pleasures of shooting grouse in Scotland is that it takes place in such beautiful surroundings and at Auchlyne, the scenery is particularly stunning. After a long afternoon, the family returns home at around six in the evening, looking forward to a hot bath in which to soothe their aching legs and a drink.

The family's sport continues in September when they start to shoot the stags. Although the hind stalking, like the bulk of the grouse shooting, is let to paying guests to boost the estate's revenue, Judy and David have made a conscious decision to keep the stags for themselves. As Judy says, 'Dave and I both feel while we've the health and strength and we both enjoy it so much, we will continue to do it, together with members of the family.'

Like grouse shooting, stalking is strenuous. The deer are spied through good field glasses or a telescope and must then be stalked with extreme stealth, until one is close enough to get a good clean shot. If there is no natural cover en route to the deer, the stalker will have to crawl through the heather or along the line of a ditch. If sheep or grouse are disturbed, they will alert the deer and the stalker will have to freeze his position – maybe for as long as half an hour – until the deer settle again. The deer must be approached upwind, because if they get even a whiff of human scent, they kick up their heels and are off. A stag may be selected for the quality of its head – the best being an 'Imperial' with at least thirteen points on its antlers – or it may be chosen because it is old and needs to be culled to improve the overall quality of the herd. The shot needs to be aimed immediately behind the stag's foreleg, so that it enters just in front of the ribs and reaches the heart.

The pleasure Judy derives from the challenge of stalking has not diminished over the years. Patience is all important and in this context she remembers one stag in particular. Much to her frustration, it was lying down in the heather as she approached it and therefore was not presenting the right target. Convinced it would get up soon, Judy waited with mounting impatience for an hour and a half, getting stiffer and more uncomfortable by the minute. Eventually she decided to try to copy the stag's roar, in an attempt to get him to move. Hearing this strange sound, he lifted his head and roared back, but still stubbornly refused to get to his feet. Judy tried squeaking her boots and blowing on grass, all to no avail. Finally, sick of lying in the damp heather, she succeeded in making a noise which resembled a sick cow. Not only did the stag get to his feet, but he started walking towards her. Closer and closer he came until Judy thought if she didn't shoot soon, he was going to walk on top of her. When he was twenty yards away, he paused for a moment and Judy steadied her aim and fired. She felt a bit sorry for him, but said later, 'On the other hand, he was a pain keeping me lying there for an hour and a half.'

October heralds cold winds, chilblains for Judy and the onset of the dark days of winter. Despite this, it is a beautiful time of year at Auchlyne as the trees turn, cloaking the glens in the rich colours of autumn. There is another Highland cattle sale and after this the hind stalking opens again on 21 October. For Judy, this is a busy time, as she and the stalker work, together with David and Emma, to get as many hinds culled as possible, before the turn of the year. Sadly, the majority of British housewives are wary of cooking game, despite the fact that it is delicious, healthy – being comparatively free of fat – and if bought from the right sources, inexpensive. As a result, much of the venison from Auchlyne and Suie used to be exported to the continent, where it was better appreciated. In recent years, however, even that market has fallen away and although some of the meat is now sold locally, Judy is getting considerably less for the venison than she used to. This has put a major dent in the estates' finances.

Christmas is a family occasion. Unfortunately, the family has now grown too large for everyone to be able to spend Christmas together, as Judy and David have five children, three son-in-laws and ten grandchildren, but a large group will gather together, either at Auchlyne or at one of the children's houses. As the year draws to a close, Judy is aware that the cycle of the seasons and the hard work which accompanies them, are about to repeat themselves. Content, however, to be back in the place she loves so much, this represents no hardship and she is determined to continue to do what she does for as long as she is able.

Considering how busy Judy is throughout the year, it is amazing that she can find time for anything else, but she has several hobbies, which she flits between as the mood takes her. She keeps a hive of sadistic bees, with whom she enjoys a love–hate relationship. A friend, knowing that Judy had been interested in bee-keeping since her teens, complained of a swarm in the attic of her house. They swarmed from the roof and whilst her friend was hosting a Sunday lunch party on her patio, Judy collected the bees from the neighbouring hedge, where they had taken refuge. Putting them in a box, she drove them home and put them in her hive. Unfortunately, they have proved to be a particularly wicked strain. They frequently chase Judy and manage to sting her whenever she tries to work in the hive, even managing to get under her veil to sting her face. To top it all, they don't even produce much honey. If pressed, Judy will reluctantly admit that they seem to have the upper hand.

More successful hobbies include making walking sticks, training her dog, making minnows for fishing, knitting and 'hammering hell' out of her electric organ, which she bought with the proceeds from a pair of her grandfather's guns, which were falling to pieces. Much as she enjoys her organ ('I like to make a noise from time to time . . .') Judy wishes she could play better, 'But I can't be bothered to learn, it would just have to happen.'

Judy enjoys all sorts of things, but only when she feels like doing them. In this way she can derive maximum enjoyment from all her varied interests. There are a few hobbies from her youth which she can no longer follow, due to the laws of the land. One of these is pearling – looking for the pearls found in freshwater mussels – in the rivers and streams which flow through Auchlyne. The tools for pearling consist of a sharp knife, a forked stick and a sort of bucket with a glass bottom. In her teens, Judy would go out in the boat and position the bucket over the water so that she could see the bottom. If she spotted the top of a likely-looking shell, she would poke it out with her forked stick and prise it open with her knife. Many times she was disappointed, but sometimes she struck lucky. On one memorable day, she managed to find two particularly good-sized pearls. These she got a jeweller to mount in a small ring, with a third oval-shaped pearl of a bluish hue which she found on another occasion.

Such treasure hunts are no longer legal, but to Judy's intense annoyance, this doesn't stop people from trying to poach pearls in her river. She found a couple one summer day, paddling about in the river and asked them what they were up to. The man was very aggressive and told her he was minding his own business and she should do the same. Naturally, this enraged Judy, who pointed out to him in no uncertain terms that this was her river – she paid rates for the fishing – and thus she had every right to enquire what they were doing. She had meanwhile spied a little glass-box contraption and knew perfectly well what they were up to. When the man came out of the water, Judy seized the box and threw it into the river. The woman flung herself in after it, making a frightful fuss and the man threatened Judy with the police for 'manhandling' him. Eventually, the pair took themselves off, cursing and swearing at Judy as they departed in their car.

Sadly, such incidents are not isolated. There is no law of trespass in Scotland and Auchlyne, like so many of the large Scottish estates, is plagued by people intent on following innocent and not so innocent ploys of their own. Although she tries to be polite, Judy becomes increasingly fed up with people who pick her mushrooms and fill the boots of their cars with her logs. Hill walkers, too, can be inconsiderate, frequently jeopardizing a day's sport from which the estate is deriving income. Judy appreciates that people want to enjoy the beauty of her hills, but wishes that they could be more considerate and tidy. It particularly worries her on stalking days, when she tries to intercept people and suggest that they go to a different part of the estate. Often she is told 'But I've come all the way from Edinburgh to climb that mountain and I'm going to do it.' As Judy says, 'Short of bashing him on the head or shooting him or something, I haven't really got a leg to stand on.'

Paperwork is another of Judy's bugbears. Nowadays, hill farms survive largely on subsidies. To be entitled to subsidies, Judy has to keep extensive and extremely time-consuming records. 'Every time we order medicine, for instance, for our sheep, we have to write in a book when we get it, from whom we get it, to what we give it, when we start giving it, when we finish giving it and how much stuff's left in the bottle at the end of it. Now when you're dealing with between three and four thousand sheep and one hundred cows, calves and heifers, you have to remember and record minute details about each animal.' The downside of owning such a magnificent estate is the worry which accompanies it. To make ends meet, Judy has had to sell off the occasional piece of ground on the outskirts of the estate as well as some of the farmhouses.

Judy has never given much thought to being a woman in her position. Her friends are a mixture of her family's social circle – consisting mainly of other landowners and childhood contemporaries – and other farmers and country people, whose company she enjoys regardless of their sex, age or status. Qualified by her experience, gained from years of dedication to the country and to country pursuits, Judy has never had a problem in exerting her authority over the men who work for her, for anyone who knows her well would not question the fact that she is fitted to run the estates by birth, by inclination and, primarily, by dint of her own efforts. It is a responsibility which she has earned.

Perhaps Judy's greatest responsibility towards Auchlyne and Suie is the question of their future. Her son Niall already has the Argaty estate, so Judy is fortunate that Emma, her eldest daughter, is keen to follow in her footsteps. Judy has already made over a large portion of Auchlyne to Emma and now they run the farms and the sporting interests between the two of them. Judy sees a lot of herself in Emma, who is a first-class shot with a rifle and a shotgun and is also a very good gillie. Eventually, Judy will hand over the whole lot to Emma, but she wants to continue to hold the reins, she says, for as long as she can without making a fool of herself. She also feels that this will give Emma more time to pick up the threads of farming.

Judy is more worried about the next generation. Neither of Emma's children seem interested in the same things that Judy was when she was their age – 'If I say, "come along, Nicola, let's go fishing," or "Richard, why don't you take your gun and go down there," they say, "we can't, we have to study" – they are much brighter than I was.' Although Richard is now such a proficient shot that he can out-perform his father on the Glorious Twelfth, he is interested in aircraft engineering, not estate management and sadly for Judy, seems destined to have a career which will lead him away from the Highlands. With a wisdom derived from years devoted to working on the land, Judy knows, however, that it is impossible to make accurate predictions about the future. For the time being, she is content in the knowledge that Auchlyne and Suie will pass down the female line, from countrywoman to countrywoman.

'I don't mind not being wealthy so long as I can keep the thing going for my daughter and grandchildren. Then I'll be quite happy – I'll have felt that I've sort of achieved something. I haven't let the side down, put it that way. And I've really had a happy life because I've done all the things I wanted to do. If I wanted a ferret, I had a ferret. If I wanted to go hunting, I went hunting and if I wanted to fish, I fished. Luckily nobody ever caught me doing something very awful so I've always been allowed to do my own thing. Spoilt rotten really . . .'

CHAPTER 2

Dawn Warr

GAMEKEEPER

D awn Warr had every opportunity in her early years to appreciate the hard physical work and long hours that gamekeeping entails. Her father was a gamekeeper and when Dawn was still in her pram, her mother would wheel her across the estate to see her father, at work in the pheasant rearing pens, and say – 'Look, there's Daddy. That's what he looks like.'

Dawn was born on 14 August 1960. Her family were living in Hampshire at the time, where her father was an under keeper to Lord Normanton on the Somerly Estate. Dawn's brothers, Harry who was then aged nine and Mick, aged seven, were not at all impressed when their mother brought Dawn back from the hospital. Mick, elected spokesperson, went to his father and pointed out that the family had been fine before Dawn came along, urging him to give her away. The boys were bitterly disappointed when he refused.

Eighteen months later, when the family moved to a picturesque estate in Cornwall, on the edge of the River Tamar, Dawn's brothers decided that as they were clearly stuck with her, they'd better bring her up as a brother. They taught her to ride a bike, to shoot and to fish with the result that she rapidly developed into a tomboy. Her efforts to keep up with her brothers and to prove that she could do whatever they could do made her extremely stubborn. From the age of two she was allowed to accompany her father, who was the estate's head keeper, in his Landrover as he went on his daily rounds. As soon as she was big enough, she helped him to clean the glass of the old hurricane lanterns which were used to keep foxes away from the pheasant poults, as well as assisting with more interesting jobs, such as feeding pheasant, catching them and clipping their wings. Although she relished these trips across the estate, as the years went by she developed a hatred of opening gates. One day when she was six years old, she had opened so many gates already, that when they pulled up at yet another one at a distant point on the estate, two or three miles from home, she said, 'I'm not opening this one.' 'Yes you are.' 'No I'm not.' 'We'll sit here then,' her father said. So they sat for quite some time, neither prepared to give way. Finally Dawn decided to leave him to it, got out of the car and walked home.

As the family lived in a fairly remote location, Dawn had to ride her pushbike for a mile each day to connect with the bus to St Mellion, which took her to Callington School. In the morning, she had to push her bike over most of the journey, as it was all uphill, but on the way home, she could freewheel the whole way. She never used her hands to steer, but leant into the corners, with the result that while she was perfecting the technique, she fell off frequently, grazing her hands, her knees and her face. On one occasion, she hit a pothole, flew over the handlebars and knocked herself out on the front wheel.

As her brothers were good shots, Dawn desperately wanted to get good enough to beat them. She was given an air-gun when she was quite young and she practised whenever she could, shooting rabbits, small birds and vermin. In the evenings, she would wait until it got dark, then sneak into one of the outbuildings and, holding a torch in one hand and her air-gun in the other, she would shoot the mice which ran up and down the walls. Desperate to be included on her brother's outings, she badgered them to take her with them, whenever they were off on some ploy across the estate. When they refused she would often try to follow them. On one occasion they threw a brick at her and cut her head open.

Frequently rejected by her brothers and not having any neighbouring children to play with, Dawn learned to be independent and to find things to do in order to keep herself amused. Returning home from school, she would go to her father's kennels and take all the working dogs out – the labradors and springer spaniels which her father used for picking up shot game, and the alsatian who was a guard dog-cum-family pet. This pack would cavort joyfully around her as she took them down to swim in the Tamar, which flowed just below the cottage. She also fished the Tamar, from the quay below the house, trying for eels, crabs, flatfish and bass. She often fished alongside her brothers who, with the benefit of the river on their doorstep, had developed into first-class fishermen. One day, wielding a worm on the end of her weighted line, she cast out and was soon wrestling with a massive eel. It put up a fierce fight – so fierce that she thought she couldn't hold on, so she yelled to Mick for help. Mick rushed over and grabbed the rod. As the battle to land it continued, they decided it was probably a conger eel. Mick was excited – from the feel of it, this leviathan would be the biggest eel that any of them had ever caught. He warmed to his task and just as he thought he was making progress, the eel wrapped its tail around a large rock on the river bottom. Mick, determined not to be beaten, tugged and tugged and at the critical moment, Dawn's knot came undone. The eel swam away and Dawn has never been forgiven.

The family household was always something of a menagerie. The children kept pets, such as dogs, rabbits and guinea pigs, but they also had a constant stream of injured or orphaned wildlife, including wild birds, crows, a fox cub, a raven called Kronk, and a squirrel called Sammy. Dawn found Sammy when he was only a few days old, on the ground underneath his dray. She attempted to climb the tree to put him back in his nest, but she couldn't reach the dray, so she tucked the tiny animal into her jumper and took him home. When she arrived, she showed off her new acquisition with great pride. Her mother was not impressed. The squirrel was covered in fleas, and as

Dawn had tucked it into her jumper, she was covered in fleas too. Both Dawn and the squirrel were liberally covered in flea powder and sent out into the garden. Because he was so tiny, Sammy had to be fed milk at regular intervals from an eye-drop dispenser. When he was older, Dawn's mother insisted that he lived outside and Dawn's father was prevailed upon to build him a cage in the garden. However, when she returned home from school each day, Dawn would collect Sammy from his cage and bring him indoors. He liked to try to mountaineer up her ankle socks and shin up her legs, clawing them in the process. Dawn didn't mind and together they worked out a number of games, the favourite of which involved the drawing-room curtains. Dawn would hold the bottom of the curtains, which were made from a silky material and Sammy would bomb up to the curtain rail. He would then position himself carefully on his stomach and, legs akimbo, slide down to Dawn. This game was repeated over and over until they tired of it and went in search of another diversion. One evening, Mick returned with a squirrel which he had shot. He took the body over to Sammy's cage and tormented him with it. 'Look at this,' he taunted maliciously. 'This is one of your ancestors!' The next time Sammy was let out of his cage, he scampered straight over to Mick and bit him. After that, he would have nothing to do with Mick. After an underkeeper had teased Sammy through the bars of his cage, Sammy extended his hatred of Mick to a hatred of all men and turned to biting them whenever he got the opportunity, although he was still fine with women. He met a sticky end when, after being with the family for two years, he escaped from his cage and was eaten by a feral cat.

One of the local tenant farmers had a fat Shetland pony called Tuppence. Dawn, keen to have a go at riding, asked if she could take Tuppence out. The farmer was more than happy to encourage her, hoping that a bit of exercise would thin Tuppence down. Tuppence had different ideas. He had to date enjoyed a life of total indolence and he had absolutely no intention of allowing this determined child to ride him out of his field. Dawn, little legs spread wide over Tuppence's ample girth, kicked and kicked, but it got her precisely nowhere. She had never had a riding lesson in her life and try as she might, she couldn't get Tuppence to budge. After many hours of frustration, she applied a little basic psychology to the situation and led Tuppence out of his field and away from the farm. She then climbed on board and Tuppence, keen to get back to the grass in his paddock, puffed his way back home. This was one solution, but to spend fifty percent of your riding time leading your pony didn't seem to Dawn to be enormously productive. Artfully, she struck up a friendship with a girl at school who had her own pony and who was, by all accounts, an excellent rider. Showing her new friend her problem with Tuppence and praising her riding skills, Dawn managed to persuade the girl to swap mounts, with the result that on all future excursions, she had a well-schooled pony to ride and Tuppence, startled from his apathy by a budding Lester Piggot, took on a new lease of life and went like stink.

While she was still too young to be allowed a shotgun, Dawn never lost the opportunity to accompany her father when he was shooting. One day, when she was about nine years old, she had a lucky escape. She had accompanied him pigeon shooting. The pigeons were coming over well and she and her father were concentrating on the flight lines. In his efforts to teach his children the basics of safe shooting, her father had always cautioned Harry and Mick about the dangers of mixing twelve-bore and twenty-bore shotgun cartridges, but somehow, absorbed in his sport, he unwittingly slipped a twenty-bore cartridge into the barrel of his twelve-bore shotgun, followed by a twelve-bore cartridge. Dawn, who had been standing behind him spotting pigeons, grew tired and sat down on the ground. The next second her father raised his gun at a pigeon passing high overhead. He fired and the barrels exploded. If Dawn had still been standing behind him, she would have borne the brunt of the explosion straight in her face. As it was, the blast had blown off part of her father's hand, so Dawn rushed to get the next shooter, telling him that her father had lost his thumb. In reality, he hadn't, but this was how it appeared to Dawn. The shooter returned with her and nearly fainted when he arrived on the scene because he couldn't stand the sight of blood. While her father was rushed to hospital, Dawn returned home to break the bad news to her mother. Keen to be the first with the news, she rushed into the house, yelling 'Mum, Mum, Dad's blown his thumb off!'

When she was twelve, her father gave Dawn her first shotgun – a little .410. He helped her to master it by teaching her how to shoot tin cans, thrown in the air. By this time, both of her brothers had left home to work as gamekeepers and Dawn already knew that she too wanted to be a keeper when she left school. In 1974 the family moved to Dorset where her father become head keeper on the Melbury Park Estate. The cottage they moved into was a beautiful, picture-postcard cottage, with a thatched roof and a stream running through the garden. The previous occupant of the cottage had allowed the flower beds to fill with weeds and the lawn to become a tangle of wild shrubs and roses. Dawn's mother, always domesticated and enthusiastically encouraged by the rest of the family – especially Dawn who, from an early age, hated domestic chores with a passion – set about turning this jungle into a proper, old-fashioned cottage garden. For a child who loved the outdoors, Melbury Park was a paradise of woodland, streams, lakes and meadows.

The only drawback from Dawn's point of view with the move to Dorset was school. She had enjoyed school in Cornwall and she had worked reasonably hard, but she hated her new school and, academically, it really set her back. When she was fourteen, her English teacher complained to her father about Dawn's lack of scholastic prowess. 'What can Dawn do?' he asked scathingly. 'Well, she can skin a deer,' her father replied. Criticism from teachers only fuelled Dawn's determination to follow in her father's footsteps and become a keeper, in which capacity, she reflected cheerfully, academic qualifications mattered not a jot. What mattered were the lessons which her father was continually teaching her as she accompanied him on his rounds – lessons such as how to identify wild birds and animal tracks and how to tell a fox den from a badger set.

Dawn left school at the earliest opportunity, when she was still fifteen. She had her sights firmly set on the position of under keeper at

Melbury. Her father was not at all keen that she should become a keeper. He had two sons who had followed in his footsteps and he did not want his only daughter to undertake such a hard existence. He considered keepering to be both unnatural and inappropriate for a woman. Much as he had enjoyed Dawn's company and help while she was growing up, he wanted her to follow a traditional feminine role and like her mother, get married, settle down, become a homemaker and start a family. Dawn was singularly unimpressed with this scenario. She had grown up with keepering and shoot days and this was all she had ever wanted. She had proved her worth against her brothers, who, due to her prowess as a shot and her stalwart toughness, had grudgingly accepted her. With characteristic stubbornness, she put in an application for the job as under keeper and was duly accepted.

She had three months grace between leaving school and starting work. At the time, her father had an under keeper, from whom she was to take over in August, so as they didn't really need her help, she spent the summer lying in the sun and generally lazing about. She also visited Harry for a short break, returning home with a tame magpie, which she had rescued from a nest when its mother was shot. This was the longest interval of leisure and laziness in her life and it was as well that she took advantage of this time, because although she thought she knew what keepering entailed, she was not fully prepared for the hard work which lay ahead of her.

When she started work she discovered that there were lots of tasks which she simply hadn't realized the position would entail. Although Dawn knew better than to accept the misconception that so many aspiring keepers labour under – namely that being a gamekeeper entails little more than walking in the woods all day with a gun over your arm – even having grown up alongside the job, she was surprised by the heavy, exhausting work which was part and parcel of her new routine. She was immediately dropped into responsibility and put in charge of three release pens, from which the young pheasant poults spread out into the woods. Her father trusted her to get on with the work in hand and apart from outlining any extra tasks which needed to be done, he largely left her to it, content in the knowledge that she would alert him if there were any problems with the pheasant. Dawn found that physically she had to build up muscles in order to carry out the daily rounds. Heavy sacks of feed had to be carried on one shoulder and gallons of water had to be lugged into the pens. If she found something too heavy or difficult, for the sake of her pride and for the sake of her father, who by rights should have had another young man as his underkeeper, she had to find a way of doing it. She needed to prove herself. Gamekeeping was what she had signed up to do and do it she would, regardless of the blood, sweat and tears it entailed.

The job had its compensations. The long, solitary hours suited Dawn's independent nature. As someone who much preferred to be outside than indoors and with a keen interest in wildlife, she relished working in the countryside on a full-time basis. She particularly enjoyed hand-feeding the poults three or four times a day and watching the deer which roamed wild in the park. Due to the regularity of her visits to feed the pheasant, the wildlife in the vicinity soon began to take her presence for granted. She found that she could get quite close to the animal and bird life and she derived great pleasure from watching their antics. She also enjoyed training her first working dog – a young springer spaniel. Up until this time the only dogs she had worked with had belonged to her father.

Unfortunately, Dawn swiftly discovered that she wasn't the only person who enjoyed walking in the woods. She frequently encountered trespassers who liked to walk their dogs through the estate and families who used the place like a public park. Human voices, children screaming and dogs – off the lead and hunting through the woods – are enormously disruptive to wildlife in general and to a shoot in particular. When pheasant poults are spreading out from the release pens they are especially vulnerable to disturbance. The Melbury Park shoot, like many others in the country, is set up in such a way that birds from a particular release pen are encouraged, by feeding, to spread to a nearby area of high ground. From here, when they are flushed for the guns, they will follow a pre-determined line over the guns, back 'home', to their release pen, where they know more food is available. This process of feeding pheasant up to the nearest elevated ground helps to ensure that the birds, when flushed, will be high-flying, sporting birds which will test the guns. Achieving the manipulation of pheasant in this way is a delicate business, and months of painstaking effort can be destroyed by a couple of uninvited dogs wreaking havoc.

On one occasion, Dawn came across two people walking in the woods right by one of the release pens. Their dog was hunting ahead of them and poults were panicking and flying everywhere. Dawn approached the couple and explained that the estate was private property and that they shouldn't be there. She added that their dog should be under control. Taking a leaf out of her father's book, she was polite but firm. The couple, however, were extremely arrogant. They said they could go where they liked and that they had no intention of leaving the estate. To prove the point, they sat down on the ground and refused to budge. As she couldn't afford to leave them alone to disturb her pheasant further, nor could she physically throw them off the place, Dawn sat down with them. After about a quarter of an hour, the woman tired of this stalemate and said 'Oh let the silly little bitch stay there!' and the pair climbed to their feet and left the estate.

Many of the objections raised by trespassers when Dawn attempted to send them off the estate, amounted to jealousy of her employer. The trespassers didn't feel it was fair for one person to own so much ground and they really believed that they should be able to go wherever they wanted to. This argument was put forward with vehemence one day by two men whom Dawn found illicitly fishing for trout on the lake. Having spotted them from a distance, she realized what they were up to and drove over to the lake. She had two Alsatians with her in the Landrover, but she realized she'd better leave them there, because if there was trouble, she could have difficulty getting both the dogs off and the trespassers could get badly bitten. Deciding, therefore, to face the men alone, she walked down to the bank and found them lurking in the brambles. There was no sign of any fishing tackle and they claimed to be bird-watching, but Dawn insisted that they had been fishing. A massive argument broke out, during which the men claimed that people could go where they liked. Dawn suggested that she could call the police to discuss the truth of this statement with them, but the men shouted her down and became more aggressive. When Dawn said she was going to search them for fishing tackle, a fracas broke out. In the end, she pushed one of the men out of the brambles. Looking at Dawn, four-square to the wind and absolutely furious, the man clearly thought better of shoving her back and together with his friend, decided to head for his car. Undeterred, Dawn followed them and took the registration number of their vehicle. In a last blistering verbal attack before they drove away, the chief protagonist said that next time he came back, he'd shoot her dogs. Livid, Dawn returned to search the brambles and found a fish, a line and a bait box.

Because they were fishing illegally, these men were technically poaching. Although Dawn had taken their vehicle registration number and had found the fish and tackle, she had not been able to hold the poachers on the estate until the police came and therefore the men could not be prosecuted. The most the police could do was to trace the owner of the car and give him a good talking to. Although such incidents are unpleasant, Dawn has always faced them head on. Encounters like these highlight the fact that she is a woman doing a man's job, but, armed with a combination of right on her side, the determination to carry out every aspect of her job to the best of her capability and – not least – a reasonable set of muscles, built up by dint of sheer hard work, Dawn is unperturbed. As she says: 'If you're dealing with a very nasty trespasser, it's no good crying, you've got to be as forceful as any man.'

On one occasion, Dawn was out on poacher patrol in the middle of the night. As she drove towards one of the estate boundaries, she noticed a red Landrover, parked in a lay-by on the main road. Her suspicions were immediately alerted, as she had been told by neighbouring keepers that there were some well-known poachers in the area at the time, who drove a red Landrover. They had the reputation of being extremely violent. Bearing this in mind, Dawn approached them in her Landrover, but decided that there was no way that she was going to get out of the car. With an eight-stone Alsatian in the back, she felt reasonably secure in the Landrover. As she got close, the poachers clearly saw her coming, because they took off down the main road toward Yeovil. Dawn took off after them. She needed to get close enough to get their vehicle registration number, so that she could log it and inform the police. Dawn chased the red Landrover as fast as she could and it took her about three miles to catch up with it and take the number. She then dropped back and headed for home. When she got back, she phoned the police and gave them the registration number. The next morning the phone rang and Dawn's father answered. It was the desk sergeant from Yeovil police station. 'I don't know what Dawn did to those poachers,' he said, 'but in the early hours of this morning, they drove into our yard in a red Landrover, which they'd stolen from the fire department and gave themselves up!'

Dawn's father had always kept Alsatians to compliment his traditional working dogs – the spaniels and labradors which are essential to most keepers. Although Alsatians are not generally perceived to be gundogs, he had found that, properly trained, they had good noses and were quite capable of helping him with tasks such as 'dogging in'. Dogging in needs to be done from September to December, the time when the pheasant are spreading out to find new territories. The purpose of it is to prevent them from spreading too far and to hold them within the estate boundaries. The keeper uses his dog to hunt out pheasant lying in an outlying area of cover and to push them on to a central area of cover, which is earmarked to be driven by the beaters.

Combined with their more widely recognized capability as guard dogs, this additional ability resulted in the Alsatians being dual purpose. At Melbury, Dawn's father had been given an Alsatian called Sabre, which was purchased for him by the estate. Shortly after being taken on as under keeper, Dawn decided that she would like an Alsatian of her own. She searched for a good bitch locally, found one with good conformation and a good temperament and arranged for Sabre, who had an excellent temperament, to be mated. It is normal after puppies have been produced for the owner of the dog to be given one puppy from the litter. This Dawn intended to buy, but Lady Theresa Agnew, who owned Melbury then, gave the puppy to Dawn as a personal present.

It was a dog puppy and Dawn named him Rebel. As well as assisting her with her work with the pheasant, part of his role would be to accompany her on poacher patrol – to help her to track poachers, to act as a deterrent and to defend her if she ran into trouble. Dawn worked hard on Rebel's training. She taught him as the police train their dogs, to track and to bite if necessary. She also taught him to respond to hand signals and to retrieve. After a while, she could throw her car keys into long grass and he would go in and find them. He would also track on a harness for over a mile. Apart from his working prowess, Rebel was also a staunch companion. Over the years, Dawn found him to be very intuitive – more of a friend than a dog, as he responded to her moods and generally cheered her up whenever she was in need of support.

Working outside every day of the year inevitably means working sometimes in really filthy weather conditions. However, because of her enthusiasm for the job, Dawn has never objected to working in pouring rain – she just dresses for it and gets on with it. She is equally tolerant of all the other negative aspects of her work. The only thing that has worried her is her back. Carrying half a hundred-weight of corn on her shoulder one day, she slipped when she was crossing a small bridge and landed on her back across a stile, with the sack of corn on top of her. This accident has left her with a recurring back problem, which worries her particularly when she is lifting heavy objects, digging holes or knocking in posts. Whilst this injury hasn't prevented her from undertaking heavy tasks, it has caused her to reflect on the strength of the female body in comparison to that of a man. Is a female body made as strongly as a man's – will hers take the degree of hammer to which she has been subjecting it, for another twenty years? To Dawn, this has been a matter of practical concern.

Despite growing up as a tomboy and embarking on a decidedly unfeminine career, Dawn enjoys getting dressed up and going out. She loves eating out and going to dances and she enjoys quite an active social life. Occasionally this is interfered with by her job. On one occasion, she donned a skirt, blouse and a pair of tights in preparation for going to a hunt dinner. She was on the point of leaving the house when the phone rang. Could she come and sort out a wounded deer which had been hit by a car on the main road? She exchanged her high heels for her wellingtons, grabbed a gun and climbed into her Landrover.

'When I jumped out of the vehicle, I could see the deer would need shooting. There were three men there and they never said a word, their mouths just sort of dropped and they obviously thought, well she's in a skirt and top and wellies. I went over and shot the deer and picked it up and threw it in the back of the Landrover and they still never said a word. I went home and my mother had to wash the blood out of my tights before I could go out.'

Over the years, Dawn has had a number of boyfriends. In her teenage years she used to get fed up with them fairly rapidly and consequently she had a different one roughly every three weeks. Those that lasted a little longer she would take home to meet her parents. Some were clearly unsuitable – when she was sixteen, she took her beau of the moment home for tea and had to hold his hand to get him past the geese. Later boyfriends she chucked because they got too serious – wanting to marry her and turn her into a housewife. The only one she ever fell seriously for unfortunately didn't feel the same way about her. In more recent years, she has had a couple of wealthy boyfriends who have proposed to her. She turned them down as she wasn't in love with them, but occasionally, when the rain has been tipping down and she's been out trying to knock a post in, she has wondered fleetingly if she made the right decision. Generally though, meeting the right man doesn't worry Dawn: 'If it happens, it happens.'

On holiday in 1984, when she was staying with Harry in North Wales, he showed her a mink and a pole cat which had been mounted by a taxidermist. Dawn was inspired and decided to have a go at taxidermy herself. As she was not at all squeamish, the goryness of skinning and boiling up skulls didn't worry her at all, so she bought a book on the subject and began to teach herself. Probably because she had spent so many hours observing animals and birds in their natural poses, she had a flair for it and even from the outset, she managed to make her specimens look quite lifelike. To her, the greatest reward was to end up with a creature which looked as if it could get up and run or fly away. As news of her talent spread further afield, people brought her unusual specimens, such as an albino badger, which had been knocked down by a car. This new outlet for her energies provided Dawn with the perfect hobby for long winter evenings.

As well as taxidermy, Dawn also enjoys painting, clay shooting – she nearly always beats her brothers now, especially if they are shooting for the traditional family stake of fifty pence – and playing skittles, which, she claims, she is not particularly good at because her bum gets in the way of her arm.

She also enjoys fishing. When Lady Theresa Agnew died, Melbury Park was passed down the female line to the Hon. Charlotte Morrison. Like Dawn, Charlotte is a countrywoman – she enjoys hunting, shooting and fishing and has always been a very good boss to Dawn. She allows Dawn to fish for the wild brown trout on the picturesque lake in the park, sometimes accompanying her during the long balmy summer evenings. After the rigours of a long day, Dawn finds fishing soothing – floating about in the boat, watching the baby ducks and coots, she can switch off for a while. She finds this gentle activity far more relaxing than sitting on a bar stool, drinking and talking to friends. During an evening in a pub, she finds either that she fidgets, looking for something to do with her hands, or that tiredness hits her, as the day's activity catches up with her.

Although she generally prefers the company of men, Dawn has two female friends, with whom she has kept in touch since her school days. She occasionally goes out for a drink with them. One of them works and the other is married with two children. The conversation is always a little difficult. As Dawn explains, 'We're on different wavelengths. They're very much into the proper way of life – children, clothes, things like that – whereas I'm much more into the animal side and working in the countryside. After a while, it's hard to make conversation. I don't mind a bit of a gossip occasionally, but I'm very different to the way they are.'

The gamekeeper's calendar has no natural break. It starts in February, after the last day of the previous shooting season. It is a time of year which Dawn looks forward to – after the pressures of three continual months of running shoots several days a week, it is a relief to have them behind her. However, without pause to catch her breath, there are jobs to which she must turn her attention immediately and the most important of these is the catching of the laying hens. Since Dawn's father started at Melbury, all the pheasant put down on the shoot have been reared from eggs produced by the park's own stock. In order to achieve this, Dawn and her father have had to run a substantial hatching and rearing programme each spring and summer. This starts with the trapping of the hen pheasant, together with a small proportion of cock birds, in catchers. The catchers are rectangular cages, 4ft × 2ft × 2ft, with a tunnel leading off one of the long sides. A trickle of corn is put down the length of the tunnel to attract the pheasant to the cage, which is heavily baited with more food. The catchers are placed in the areas where the pheasant are normally fed and their daily food ration is reduced to make them keener to enter the tunnels.

The catchers are checked five times a day and the good quality healthy hens, together with the best of the cock pheasant, are transferred to holding pens. The remainder are released. From the holding pens, the breeding stock are transferred to laying pens, but first these pens must be made ready. Electric fencing has to be run around the bottom of the pens to discourage foxes from digging in and nest boxes and weather protection has to be placed inside the pens. The hens have to be brailled to stop them from flying. One wing is tied in a comfortable, folded position with the aid of a special piece of soft tape. Before being released into the pens, the hens are also fitted with 'specs' – little pieces of plastic which clip painlessly into their nostrils, with tiny hoops which stand up in front of their eyes, preventing them from eating their own eggs.

The job Dawn hates most in her year falls in February and early March – the cleaning and scrubbing of incubators and rearing equipment. All the incubators and hatchers have to be disinfected, tested and any necessary maintenance carried out. This amounts to unrelieved tedium of an arduous nature, but it is an essential job, as either infection or malfunction in an incubator once eggs are installed, can result in the loss of many hundreds of chicks.

In March, work must start on the release pens, because once the eggs start to go into the incubators, there will be no time to do this as the weeks pass in a frenzied blur of activity, up until the time when the six- to seven-week-old poults are ready to go out into these specially prepared and carefully positioned enclosures. Old release pens need to be repaired – any holes in the netting must be patched and trees or branches which have fallen through part of the perimeter removed. The vegetation inside them needs to have tracks cut through it, which serve as open areas, or 'feed rides', where corn can be scattered. Sprucing up old pens is generally quite quick to do, but if new pens need to be built, this is seriously hard work. Once the ideal area for the pen has been identified, holes have to be dug at regular intervals for the posts and the route cleared through trees and other obstructions for 6-ft netting to be run around the perimeter. The netting has to be turned out around the bottom by 12″ and pegged down to prevent predators from digging in. Another band of 3-ft netting has to be run round the top to achieve the right height, in order to make the pens as vermin-proof as possible. These two runs of netting have to be painstakingly laced together. One of the biggest release pens that Dawn constructed was 2,300 feet around the perimeter. This she built with the help of two lads, in just nine days.

When the pens are completed, electric fences must be run round the outside and feed rides have to be cut through the vegetation, fifty to a hundred yards beyond the pens. When the pheasant come out of the release pens and start to spread out across the park, their corn is scattered further away every day and they are called with a whistle to encourage them to wander further from the pen, until they come across the feed rides. These are strewn with straw to keep the pheasant occupied, as they scratch around in it to find their food.

The physical work that Dawn undertakes as part of her job often necessitates working with men. When she was younger, Dawn used to encounter some resentment from other women in the community, who were clearly concerned about their men working alongside Dawn. They seemed unable to grasp the fact that men volunteered to help Dawn because they actually enjoyed the work, not because she was a woman. To Dawn, the greatest compliment that her male helpers could pay her was not to treat her as a female. 'Rather than actually holding the gate open and saying "I'll hit that post, Dawn, not you," we work together. They don't class me as a woman on this place – they just class me as one of the team.'

Dawn's manual labour during this period has traditionally been enlivened by two events. The first of these is a clay shoot which takes place annually on the estate. Dawn instigated this event some years ago. She suggested that teams consisting of five men (or women), should be invited, from all over the south and south west, to come to Melbury to take part in a competition, from which all the proceeds would go to charity. The event proved to be extremely popular and went from strength to strength, with up to fifty-five teams shooting during the day. Although it requires a lot of organization, Dawn has always thoroughly enjoyed the day. It has also been worthwhile for the charities – over the years the money generated has escalated to a couple of thousand pounds. In 1993, Dawn beat all her male colleagues to win the keeper's shooting prize.

The other high spot in the early months of Dawn's year is her annual holiday. This has to fit around the job, because there is no way that the job can fit around it. Consequently, Dawn has not had a summer holiday in all the years that she has been keepering. A few years ago, she went to Tenerife for a couple of weeks. Despite her worldly common sense and practical abilities, Dawn is not at all widely travelled. It was her first time on a aeroplane and indeed, her first time out of the country. She enjoyed it, but she felt that fourteen days was too long to be away and she missed her dogs. However, she enjoyed going abroad more than she enjoyed her only trip to London. An artist friend invited her to town to see an exhibition of his pictures. After the exhibition, Dawn spent the night with friends. Before catching the train back to Dorset the following day, she went exploring on her own, to see Harrods and museums and all the sights which she had read about but never seen. After tramping the pavements for some hours, she was very relieved to climb on to the train and return to the peace of the Dorset countryside. Her verdict when she got home was that there were 'an awful lot of people' and that she found walking on pavements particularly tiring.

Any little diversions and excursions come to an abrupt end during the first week of April, when the pheasant start to lay. The eggs have to be collected from the laying pens three times a day and stored at room temperature, until there is a batch large enough to be put into an incubator. Before this the eggs have to be washed in disinfectant, to prevent them from carrying any bugs into the incubators. The majority of game farms clean their eggs in an automatic egg washer, but Dawn prefers to do it by hand, in a bucket. By handling each egg, she can ensure that it is properly washed and she can also pick out any which have cracks or faults in the shell. She will continue to collect eggs until mid-June, so the incubation season is fairly protracted, with batch after batch of eggs being incubated and hatched at different stages. When Dawn has enough eggs, the three hundred odd hens have their brailles and specs removed and they are released back into the park, together with the forty or so cock birds which have been with them. Usually, the hens will then make their own nests in the wild and lay again.

When the eggs start to hatch, Dawn's life begins to get really hectic. 'A pheasant chick,' she says, 'from day one, has one ambition – to commit suicide as early in life as possible.' They need unstinting care and attention right from the egg. Whilst transferring the early chicks from the hatchers to the brooders in the rearing field, Dawn still has to continue to bring in eggs from the laying pens and now she also has two lots to feed. When the poults are three weeks old, they will be quite mobile and will be allowed to roam up and down the full length of the 48 ft long × 4 ft wide rearing runs. At this point, they must be caught up and fitted with 'bits'. Bits, like specs, are made from plastic and clip into the nostrils. They take the form of a miniature ring which is inserted into the poult's mouth, in such a way that the mouth is held just open. The purpose of this is to prevent the poults from plucking each other. Young pheasant get very bored confined in the rearing pens and left to their own devices, will help to alleviate this boredom by seizing a companion's plumage in their beak and savagely plucking out the feathers, drawing blood. With their beaks held open a fraction of an inch by the bits, they are unable to get a purchase on the feathers.

By this stage, the ground beneath the rearing runs is becoming quite soiled, so all the runs must be picked up and moved to fresh ground. Thereafter, the runs are moved weekly until early July, when the poults are six or seven weeks old. At this age, provided the weather is good enough, the poults can be put into the release pens. Dawn tries to pick a sunny day to move them, so that they feel a sense of well-being and will settle down in their new environment quickly. Before they are moved, their bits are taken out and one wing is clipped, to prevent them from flying out of the release pen, over the wire perimeter. For the first couple of days the poults are put into a smaller pen within the main release pen, until they are used to being fed with corn scattered by hand. To attract their attention, Dawn whistles to them to call them over for food. Once they are responding to the whistle, they are let out of the small pen, to have the run of the release pen.

When the poults are between twelve and fourteen weeks old, their feathers have regrown sufficiently for them to be able to fly out over the top of the release pen perimeter. Dawn feeds them daily in the feed rides and by this stage, she admits to having a few favourites. 'There are always certain pheasants which have character, so I think there are always favourites on the feed ride, but nearly always your favourites are the first ones that get shot, so it never pays to be a favourite.'

Long before they face the guns, the pheasant will face other hazards. Given the opportunity, predators will pick off poults at any age and stage. Foxes, mink, stoats, feral cats and a host of others need to be controlled if Dawn's pheasant are to make it through the autumn. The avian predators she shoots and traps in large box cages called larsen traps. As well as reducing the predation on pheasant poults, this also helps the song-bird population, which suffers from the raids which these aerial bandits will carry out on eggs and nestlings. By far the greatest problem, though, are foxes. A fox will kill not just out of hunger, but for the sake of killing and there are few sights more upsetting for a keeper first thing in the morning than a dozen dead pheasant with their heads taken off, which have fallen prey to a fox during the previous night. Despite the necessity to protect her poults, Dawn has a problem with fox control. Charlotte Morrison, her employer, enjoys hunting. When hounds meet at Melbury, the hunt expects to find foxes, so Dawn has to do her best to identify and deal only with the foxes that trouble her pheasant, leaving the rest alone.

After the rigours of the rearing season, August is a quieter month, when the rearing equipment can be packed away and smaller jobs carried out, such as constructing butts around the flight ponds in preparation for duck shooting, which starts in September. By September the pheasant are widely spread across the estate, so Dawn starts to dog them in with the aid of Rebel and her other working dogs. By October, her attention is firmly focused on fine tuning arrangements for the shooting season, which is now imminent. Although the season for pheasant opens on 1 October, they are not shot until the month end, as they are not sufficiently developed to fly well enough to be sporting until late October at the very earliest. Dawn will spend her time setting numbered pegs to mark the spots where the guns will stand for each drive and stringing out lines with plastic strips hanging from them at the flushing points, to encourage the pheasant to take off. During the last week of October, she will have the first shoot, which is only a small day in terms of the number of pheasant which will be shot.

The first big day will be in early November. The guests arrive at the main house at about 9.15 a.m. and draw numbers for their pegs, which will determine their position in the line of guns. Usually, a team for a day's driven pheasant shooting consists of eight guns. The pegs are positioned for each drive in such a way that the pheasant should pass over the guns as high as possible. In theory, the guns at the middle pegs should get the most shooting, although it doesn't always work out this way. Every drive – and there will usually be six or seven in a day – the guns move up three pegs, so the best shooting positions are distributed amongst them as fairly as possible. On a shoot day, the keeper has a lot to co-ordinate, but the most important task is to run the beating line. Dawn generally has somewhere in the region of thirty beaters, a number of whom work their own dogs within the line. The beaters' job is to walk in a line through the woods and cover crops, pushing the pheasant out from the cover in such a way that they fly over the guns. Beaters are paid a small amount for their services, but the majority don't turn out for the money, but for the pleasure of being out in the country for the day, amid an atmosphere of camaraderie. There are exceptions, however. Dawn once found a 'stop' asleep under a tree. A stop is a person who is strategically positioned with a stick, to tap on a tree or fence post constantly during a drive, to dissuade pheasant from passing him and hence from leaving the drive. When the sleeping stop was woken up by a very angry Dawn, he made matters worse by saying that if he had remembered to bring a book, he wouldn't have fallen asleep. He was clearly out just for the money, with no intention of doing a proper job, so he was sent home.

Once the guns are in position, the drive starts. It is the keeper's task to pace the beating line so that the pheasant are trickled out slowly, rather than allowing too many to be flushed at one time. Dawn co-ordinates the line by radio and, she claims, by merit of her loud voice. She enjoys running the beating line and although she puts up with a lot of good-natured teasing from the men working alongside her, nobody questions her authority. As well as beaters, she has to organize the stops and the pickers up, who use dogs to retrieve the shot birds. At the end of the day, the shot birds are counted and put in the larder and Dawn cleans all the guns before the guests take them home. Shoot days are long and tiring, but Dawn has never been anxious about a day. She knows that she has prepared as thoroughly as possible and that worrying won't help. Instead, she makes every effort to ensure that both guns and beaters enjoy their day. If the guns appreciate the day, this is reward enough for her efforts.

'I think the majority of guns don't realize actually how much work has gone through the whole year for that one day's shooting. They always say thank you if I see them – perhaps because they're frightened of me because my voice carries so much! But it's always nice to hear them say how nice a day was and how much they've enjoyed it – at the end of the day it makes it all worthwhile.'

The shoots continue through until 1 February, usually numbering somewhere in the region of twenty-four, including boundary days. Boundary days are smaller 'walked-up' days, where three or four guns, with Dawn and the dogs, will walk round the boundaries, shooting any game which they can flush in their path. On the last day of the season, there is a beaters' day, when all the regulars from the beating line are treated to a driven day. Because there are more than the usual number of eight guns, the pegs on the drives are shared out equally throughout the day, while those who aren't shooting a particular drive, beat. This day is followed a week later by a beaters' party to round off the season. Dawn looks forward to this each year – it is normally a riotous occasion with a lot of good natured banter and energetic dancing.

In March 1993, Dawn's father retired from his position as head keeper and Dawn, who had been under keeper for eighteen years, took over. She became unique – the only female head keeper in the country. It had always been understood that she would take over one day and she had certainly earned the position. Her father's health had been slowly deteriorating, as the years of hard physical work took their toll and Dawn had been gradually doing more and more. She had been running the beating line for quite a few years, ever since her father had been unable to walk for the fifteen to twenty miles which beating entails. She took over the position of head keeper with a mixture of personal pride and relief for her father, who, after forty years as a keeper, could now sleep late in the mornings, take a summer holiday and generally enjoy a well-earned rest.

The new position inevitably amounted to an increased workload. It was never suggested that Dawn should have an under keeper – as far as the estate was concerned she seemed perfectly capable of coping on her own, so she absorbed the tasks that her father had been doing on top of her own. Her only help was on Saturdays, when two of the beaters came to help her with any particularly heavy work, or any jobs which required more than one person. They gave their time freely, in return for an excellent lunch, cooked by Dawn's mother. Dawn's father, suddenly faced with unaccustomed time on his hands, found it extremely hard to relax and he persisted in getting up early, but he did have a summer holiday and with Dawn living under the same roof, he retained all his interest in the job, without actually having to do it.

Despite the increased workload, Dawn was happy. Most head keepers, newly promoted, would be worried about their first shoot, but Dawn, with her easygoing, sunny disposition, sailed through it without a moment's anxiety. At the end of a very good day, she was able, as head keeper, to go up to the big house for the first time on a shoot day, to take the guests their brace of pheasant each and to report on the total bag. She was proud to be introduced to people as the head keeper – she had always enjoyed the surprise on people's faces when they learned that she was a gamekeeper. She found it was a nice kick to be the only woman in a man's world. Sadly, her pleasure in her new position was to be short-lived.

In late 1993 there were some changes in management at Melbury Park, the most significant one of which, from Dawn's point of view, was that a shoot manager was put over her. In many respects, this appeared to be something of an insult. Dawn knew the estate like the back of her hand. She was a highly experienced keeper, who strove constantly to improve the quality of her drives and spared no effort on behalf of her employer. She also enjoyed an excellent relationship with her regular team of beaters and pickers up. No sooner had she taken over the position of head keeper – a position for which she had worked hard for many years – than she was belittled by being put under an outsider.

Swallowing her hurt pride, Dawn decided to do her best to work with the new manager. She showed him round the park, explaining how the drives worked and what her plans were for the next season. Her new boss had his own ideas. He outlined to Dawn the changes which he wanted her to instigate – which included radical alterations. Dawn was not at all convinced that these changes would be for the best. He even questioned the amount of feed which the pheasant were consuming over the course of the year, announcing his intention to calculate the optimum amount of corn per bird, per annum. Dawn tried to explain that the equation was not a simple one – sometimes she needed to feed lightly and sometimes she needed to feed very heavily, in order to achieve a particular concentration or pattern of movement. He did not support this view.

Dawn struggled to come to terms with this new development. One minute, she had effectively been her own boss, wholly responsible for the quality of the shoots and for the efforts which went into ensuring that quality. Now, she was in an invidious position. If she followed the instructions of her new manager and the next shooting season was a good one, he would take the credit. If, however, the season was bad, as she strongly suspected it would be, she would undoubtedly take the blame. Moreover, she had no desire to see the superb shoot which she had built up with her father spoiled, spoiling with it her own reputation. She decided that she had no choice but to hand in her resignation.

She gave the estate three months' notice. The decision to leave was not taken lightly. When her father retired, her parents had stayed on with her in the beautiful thatched keeper's cottage, which had been their home for twenty years. Now they would have to move to a smaller tied cottage on the estate. In the short term, Dawn would have to move with them too. She would also have to decide what she was going to do in the future. Getting another job as a keeper seemed an unlikely option. The chances of finding an estate which would have the courage to employ a woman as a head keeper were slim, however well qualified that woman might be. For every keepering position which comes up, there are literally hundreds of male applicants, some of whom are just as well qualified as Dawn, so she was realistic enough to know that this particular deck was stacked against her.

She faced her future philosophically. The keeper's job had been hard. She had been out in all weathers and she had earned very little money. Her back still played her up when she had to do heavy work and she had been anxious for some years about whether she would be physically capable of doing the job until she was sixty. It was nice to think that she wouldn't have to build those two release pens single-handed that spring and the thought that shortly she would be able to have a lie-in in the morning was not unattractive either. If she harboured any doubts about leaving, she only had to look at the other employees on the estate to know that she had made the right decision. All around her she saw changes in the estate and in the people who worked there. In her eyes, from a community who had worked together like a family, they had become individuals who, in fear of their jobs, suddenly had no time to help anyone else on the estate. Moreover, Dawn had her self-respect to consider – she had always spoken her mind and she wouldn't be trodden on, now or in the future.

What the future holds for Dawn is not certain. Amongst her ambitions, she wants to own her own house – preferably one with central heating, which would be an unaccustomed luxury – and she would like her own business. With her talent for taxidermy and an ability to paint and sketch, she entertains thoughts of going self-employed and attempting to make her living by selling paintings and mounted specimens. If she can manage to make ends meet in this way, she stands some chance of being able to preserve herself from the rat-race and remain true to her vocation as a countrywoman. If she can, she would also like to find a piece of ground on which she could run a do-it-yourself shoot – mainly for those who have so enjoyed helping her with the shoot over the years at Melbury. Above all, she wants what she has had – freedom of choice and the chance to continue to work in the countryside which she loves so much. This she values much more highly than money.

'Being able to work in the environment – with the animals and the birds and almost being free – I suppose you could class it as something extra special and not that many people can do it. It gives you more than being rich could ever give you.'

CHAPTER 3

Katy Cropper

―――――――――――――

SHEPHERDESS

Katy Cropper married a professional dog handler on April Fool's Day, wearing her wellington boots under her wedding dress. She was twenty-three years old and this was her second marriage. Throughout her young life, she had been a rebel. From a naughty, precocious child, she had grown into a volatile, feckless teenager, yet there had always been one stabilizing force in her life – her love of animals. When she went to her first sheepdog trial in 1982, her desire to devote herself to working with animals crystallized and took shape. This resulted in a partnership between Katy and sheepdogs which has enriched her life immeasurably and has drawn her inextricably into the male-dominated world of sheep and shepherding.

Katy was born on 25 February 1961 in Clatterbridge, Cheshire, where her father was the deputy headmaster of a boys' school. When she was four her parents moved to Wales, to found St David's College at Gloddaeth Hall, near Llandudno. Already they could see that Katy was the only one of their five children who threatened to be a non-conformist. In an effort to give her the best possible education, they sent her to Penrhos College in Colwyn Bay – a public school for the education of young ladies. Unfortunately, Katy was no young lady. Despite her parents' best efforts to the contrary, she was a wilful, unruly tomboy and consequently she and Penrhos College were not a happy match.

She was always in trouble – a fact born out by her school reports. These described her variously as 'Erratic', 'Untidy', 'Disruptive' and 'A disgrace to herself and the school'. Unless lessons included something to do with animals, she made no effort whatsoever to apply herself to the business of learning. Worse, she applied her vivid imagination to thinking up illicit ploys and leading other pupils astray. Her only saving grace from the school's point of view was that she excelled at sports and athletics. Naturally competitive, she was prepared to work hard to win and win she did, with the result that she competed not just at school level but also for the Amateur Athletic Association, for Clwyd County and for the British Amateur Gymnastic Association. She ran the 1500 metres for Wales. While her fellow competitors trained on running tracks with proper shoes and spikes, Katy trained by running over the fields every night in whatever footwear she had on at the time. She gave a race everything she'd got, tucking in behind the leader the whole way round, then, on the last lap, going like a bat out of hell, taking the lead just in time to cross the finishing line first. After a race, she would flop down, completely exhausted and unable to move for about an hour. Although she could never be prevailed upon to exert herself similarly in her studies, her sporting achievements gave her a degree of celebrity at school which helped to compensate for her notoriety in the classroom.

Katy had a passion for ponies. Her parents allowed her to take lessons at a local riding school in Wales, but she yearned for a pony of her own. In the middle of the night, she would sneak out of the house and head down the road to a nearby field which contained a mule and some ponies. Throwing a rope around the neck of a pony, she would ride it bareback, galloping round and round the field, exulting in a heady sense of freedom. One night, she persuaded her younger sister Ali to accompany her and the poor child got severely bitten in the chest by the mule. Katy bullied Ali into silence and when the tooth-marks were discovered by their mother, Katy denied any knowledge of the incident. However, her nocturnal forays came to an abrupt end when her mother caught her leaving the house one night, clothed in her pyjamas and a pair of wellington boots.

Eventually Katy's parent succumbed to pressure and bought Katy a succession of ponies of her own, which she took to the local pony-club meetings and rode energetically in gymkhanas. Besotted with animals in general and horses in particular, Katy may have neglected her school work but she never neglected her animals. They evoked in her a heightened sense of protectiveness towards all creatures and she abhorred anything which her young mind perceived as cruelty. Her parents leased Gloddaeth Hall from Lord Mostyn, who owned all the surrounding land. Katy was the bane of his gamekeeper's existence, as she galloped her pony wildly through the fields and woods on shoot mornings, scattering the pheasant to the furthest corners of the estate in her attempts to save them. One afternoon she accompanied her parents to tea with Lord Mostyn. Prowling around his drawing room while the adults were drinking tea and chatting politely, she came across a paperweight made from the hoof of a horse. To the acute embarrassment of her parents, she made a tremendous scene and had to be taken home.

As a teenager, Katy whiled away her school holidays going to the pony club and galloping her ponies at top speed over the surrounding countryside. Her sisters all had holiday jobs and in an effort to make her more responsible, her father told the thirteen-year-old Katy that she must also find work for the summer. In response to this pressure, she purchased a horse and cart from a gypsy. The first her father knew of her fledgling efforts in the world of commerce was when someone went into his office to inform him that they had just seen his daughter going down the street yelling, 'Rag and bone!' Katy was thereafter permitted to spend the rest of the summer idling away her time, as before.

When she became interested in boys, St David's College provided a never-ending supply. She would claim to be going for a ride and take her pony into the woods to meet her latest boyfriend. At the age of fourteen, she regularly joined up with a crowd of boys in the local pub, getting absolutely plastered on cider. Her parents despaired and remonstrated with her constantly over incident after incident, but it had not the slightest effect. Finally, in desperation, they took her to see a psychiatrist, but he too stubbed his toe on Katy, who could see no point in his questions and cried until she was taken home.

Only two people exerted any influence over Katy in her youth. One was her first serious boyfriend, Charlie, with whom she went out for about two years. He was blonde and extremely good-looking – the son of a Cambridge farmer. Eventually he dumped her and Katy, who had imagined that they would be together forever, was heartbroken. She vowed that no man would ever hurt her again like Charlie and from that day to this, she has always been the one who has ended a relationship the minute it appeared to be on stony ground. The other person who had a profound affect on Katy was her nanny, Patricia Wright. Trish, as she was known to the family, gave Katy unstinting love and affection which Katy returned in equal measure. Trish eventually became the matron at St David's, where she was respected by staff, pupils and parents alike for her larger-than-life personality and her good humour. With her uncritical, affectionate nature, she was the rock to whom Katy could anchor herself when she had managed to alienate everyone else around her with her irresponsible, irrepressible behaviour.

Katy left school at the age of eighteen with few qualifications and no plans. She had spent her latter school holidays helping out on local farms and she would have liked to find work on a farm, but there was none available. She helped out at a zoo for six weeks' work experience, but after that she was unable to find other work with animals. While she had been at school, art was the only thing other than sport in which she had shown any prowess, so her father encouraged her to apply for a year's foundation course at an art college in York. To her surprise, the college accepted her, but although she stuck the course for the year, she quickly realized that she did not have an artistic vocation and she marked time restlessly. Her year was not helped by the news that Trish, aged only forty-nine, was dying of cancer. Katy rushed back to St David's and saw her just before she died. The funeral was held in the church next door to the college and Katy wept loudly and inconsolably throughout. She had lost her rock and without it, she felt as if she had been set adrift, with no sense of direction or purpose.

Shortly after Trish's death, Katy returned from art college to Llandudno, feeling unhinged and unhappy, and still with no ideas about her future. From her parents' point of view, the only consolation at this time was that Katy had for once attached herself to a boy of whom they approved. His name was Amos and he farmed ground in Anglesey for his parents. Although this relationship pleased them it did not solve the problem of how Katy was to spend her time. In an attempt to find suitable summer employment for her, her father showed her a brochure about Camp America – a USA-based company which runs children's summer camps.

Katy was rather taken with the idea of spending the summer in the States while she dwelt on her future, so she travelled to Camp Four Winds on the coast of Maine, to supervise the teaching of arts and crafts. The majority of the children staying there attended boarding school in term time and were pitched off to camp to get them out of their parent's way in the school holidays. Consequently, some were suffering from feelings of rejection and Katy, with her persistent alienation from her own parents, could relate to these feelings. This empathy with the children highlighted her own feelings of misery and frustration and at the end of the summer she returned to Wales having failed to make any decision about her future.

Amos, however, had evidently missed her vibrant and energetic presence and shortly after her return, he proposed. Thrilled at the thought of becoming a farmer's wife, Katy accepted with alacrity. Both sets of parents were delighted at the match and when Amos's parents gave them the farm on Anglesey, which Amos had been managing, as a wedding present, the couple's future seemed secure.

Initially, Katy and Amos were happy enough. Katy had been

nursing a secret yearning to become involved in sheep and shepherding for some time and now she had an outlet for her ambition. Together, they built up their flock of Welsh half-bred ewes and, with the aid of advice from local farmers and some good books, they struggled through their first lambing season. It was an eye-opener for Katy, as she began to grasp the realities of the saying 'When you have livestock, you have deadstock.' Not only did they lose stock through the inevitable instances of illness or misfortune, but to Katy's horror, they also lost some due to her own mismanagement. She killed an orphaned lamb with kindness by overfeeding it from a bottle and whilst carrying another, she broke its leg by trapping it between her own legs while walking too quickly. These incidents brought home to Katy the harsh realities of farming and animal husbandry.

Although she gradually came to terms with the ups and downs of farming, Katy could not come to terms with the fact that despite having achieved the lifestyle which she thought she wanted, she was still unhappy. She loved working on the farm, but the confines of marriage did not suit her. She felt stifled. Increasingly a little voice at the back of her head urged her to kick over the traces and break free. Finally, although she was aware of the wounds she would inflict on Amos and on both sets of in-laws, she walked away from her husband and her life in Anglesey after just one year of marriage.

Thus it was that a strange menagerie ended up in a caravan on another farm in Anglesey. When she left Amos, Katy, now aged twenty-two, took with her a nanny-goat called Horlicks, a gander called Gandhi with his retinue of geese, and a sheepdog of dubious pedigree called Sykes. Katy had struck a deal with Emlyn Roberts, who ran sheepdog training classes for the Agricultural Training Board, to allow her and her animals to take up residence in his caravan, in return for looking after ten sows and helping with his sheep. She found the pigs to be great characters and she grew particularly fond of one piglet who rejoiced in the name of Porky. Apart from possessing an endearing personality, Porky's principle claim to fame was that he could round up sheep with much more proficiency than Sykes.

Sykes was not a pure Border Collie. He had been sired by a sheepdog called Bill, which Amos and Katy had acquired to help with their flock of Welsh half-bred ewes. Katy had decided to get herself a puppy to train after she had been to see her first sheepdog trial. Realizing that she needed help if she was ever to make the grade with sheepdogs, Katy had attended the Agricultural Training Board classes and this is where she had met Emlyn. Ensconced in her caravan, having turned her entire life on its head, the one thing Katy was now certain of was that she desperately wanted to succeed in the competitive world of sheepdog trialling.

Like her sport at school, she was really prepared to work at it. Unfortunately, however, neither she nor Sykes was the ideal raw material. To start with, she was completely the wrong temperament to work with sheepdogs. The minute things began to go astray, instead of attempting to rectify the situation calmly, Katy would get excited and start shouting. This in turn would upset Sykes and the sheep would swiftly get out of control. In addition, Sykes was far from the definitive sheepdog. He had little natural ability and no real herding instinct. In terms of serious competitive trialling, therefore, they were doomed from the start, but this didn't stop Katy from trying and soon the duo became a familiar sight at all the small sheepdog trials across the length and breadth of Wales.

The combination was the cause of some mirth amongst the experienced dog handlers. With Katy on the field, there was never a dull moment. If she wasn't bawling at Sykes in desperation, she was on her knees pleading with him to get it right. Together they would rush things, invariably ending up with a flock of out-of-control sheep careering wildly around the trialling field. Meirion Jones, one of the best handlers in the British Isles and twice winner of the prestigious International Supreme Championship, suggested to Katy that after Sykes had made his initial outrun to the back of the sheep, she should drop him – get him to lie down – and then count to ten before asking him to lift the sheep – start moving them forward. Taking on board this suggestion at the next trial, Katy dispatched Sykes on his outrun, full of good intentions. After the outrun she managed to drop him –

something he was good at – and obediently she counted to ten. Unfortunately, the sheep didn't want to count to ten and they set off down the field on their own at a hell of a pace. Storming past an appalled Katy, they disappeared into the refreshment tent, from whence shrieks and screams of consternation and the odd crash could be heard. Unperturbed, Meirion strolled up to Katy and said: 'Try counting to four next time.'

Amused by this feisty, energetic girl who had burst on to their trialling scene with her noise and enthusiasm, all the trainers tried to advise her. With one voice they told her to sell Sykes and get herself a puppy from registered working stock, with which she would stand some chance of success. Katy stubbornly refused to take their advice. She was convinced she could succeed with Sykes and she devoted two years to his training. She bought her own sheep to practise with and she continued with the ATB training classes. With relentless determination she filled every spare minute of her day with sheepdogs and sheep and they became her obsession, as she struggled to get inside Sykes' head in an effort to read him and compensate for his faults. Slowly but surely, they both improved.

In 1984, she took Sykes to a trial near Caernarfon. As usual, it was the kind of trial which anyone could enter, as she and Sykes were not in the league of being able to qualify for the more important national trials. The trial was held in a big flat field, dotted with rushes. There were approximately one hundred competitors – mostly Welsh sheepdog men. When her turn came, Katy walked out with Sykes, prepared, as usual, for anything to go wrong. However, she made a determined effort to take things calmly and to her delight, Sykes went really well, handling his sheep with precision and completing well within the allotted time. Their score was a good one, but with such a large number of competitors, Katy had to wait nervously until the end of the competition to see if they would be beaten. It was destined to be their day and after the last competitor had left the field, Katy and Sykes were announced as the winners. Thrilled to bits, a jubilant Katy collected her trophy.

Emlyn's father John gave Katy a border collie puppy which she named Bonky Bill. Sadly, the dog lived up to his name and Katy was saddled with another sheepdog blessed with little or no natural ability. Undeterred, she threw herself into his training, meanwhile continuing to take Sykes to as many trials as possible. In 1984, she went to a trial at Bala in Wales. Some of the best sheepdog handlers in the country were there, including Jim Cropper, whom Katy had heard a great deal about, but never seen in action. He had the reputation of disappearing into the nearest pub during a trial, while all the other competitors remained glued to every run, concentrating intently in preparation for their own turn. When Jim's turn came, he would emerge from the pub, go straight to the post, run his dog perfectly and win. Katy was intrigued.

From the moment she saw him take the field, Jim impressed her. This giant of a man with wavy blondish hair, strode to the post and whistled so quietly to his dog that it was barely audible. As the run progressed, it was as if he had cast a spell over both dog and sheep. He didn't use his voice once as his dog brought the sheep straight to him. It was magical to watch. After the run, Katy went over and introduced herself and spoke to his dog, Lad, who, at the age of four, was just coming into his prime and was tipped as a likely winner of the coveted International Championship in the years ahead. Katy and Jim talked at length and they promised to meet again at the British Subaru Championship Trial in Ruthin a few weeks later.

The Subaru trial always has a massive entry, with upwards of 370 dogs running in it. Katy, who had entered the trial for the last two years, came nowhere, but Jim, with another spellbinding performance, won it outright with Lad. When Katy went to find him afterwards, full of questions and admiration, Jim told her that if she really wanted to learn about dogs, she would have to come and stay with him. Delighted, Katy accepted and they arranged that Jim would pick her up in a few weeks' time, together with Sykes and Bill.

In the intervening weeks, Jim phoned Katy one evening with devastating news. Lad had been found hanging from some fencing by one of his back legs and the leg was so badly damaged that Jim had to face the choice of having the leg amputated or having Lad put down. Katy was horrified. Lad had such talent and ability, it was unthinkable that this brilliant dog could be put down. She pleaded with Jim to give him a chance, 'Let me have him and get him back to full health again – I'll keep him as a pet.' With some reservations, Jim agreed. Shortly afterwards he travelled to pick up Katy and her dogs, to take them back to his house in Rossendale, Lancashire for a week or so of training. He forewarned Katy that this would be aimed principally at her, not the dogs. Little did Katy realize that she would not return home for three years.

When she arrived at Rossendale, Jim's entire family, including his three children from his previous marriage who were around Katy's age, trooped into the house to meet her. Clearly Jim had told them quite a lot about her and they were curious to see her in the flesh. On the domestic front, the house was spartan to say the least – it was almost completely devoid of home comforts and freezing cold. Neither Jim not Katy were particularly good cooks, but Katy, eager to impress, made an effort and Jim could churn out a strange but tasty concoction consisting of vegetables, eggs, oats and cheese, fried up together in a colourful stodge. Although home life was far from luxurious, Katy hadn't come for a holiday, she'd come for Jim's wisdom and for the dogs. Her enthusiasm remained undaunted and it was an added bonus that she was falling in love.

Her lessons in handling dogs progressed well, but Jim urged her to be much firmer with Bill and Sykes. However, even under his expert guidance, there was little that could be done to improve these two. Comparing them unfavourably with the other sheepdogs in Jim's kennels, Katy reluctantly had to admit to herself that she might have to sell them and start again. Her mind was made up for her when Sykes went next door and worried a neighbour's sheep. This was the final straw and she sold both him and Bill. She also realized that her habit of leaving her dogs loose to roam around was irresponsible and in future she kennelled all her dogs. Meanwhile, Lad was progressing well after his traumatic operation, as Katy devotedly nursed him back to health. To speed up his convalescence, she took him for long walks over the fell. As she walked, she mused on his recovery – considering the severity of his accident and the ensuing surgery, he was coping with his disability remarkably well. High on the fell one afternoon, she spied some sheep in the distance. Curious as to his reaction, she said, 'Come bye, Lad.' To her astonishment, he went off at a fair old lick, lifted the sheep and without a further word of instruction brought them back to her. From his face, she could see that he had enjoyed the exercise hugely.

Katy couldn't believe her luck. From apparently being the owner of a cripple – whom she had taken on out of the goodness of her heart – she had suddenly and unexpectedly found that she in fact owned a dog of extraordinary quality. Moreover, when Lad was running, you couldn't see that he only had three legs. His ability seemed undiminished and as a partnership, they had the added advantage that during Lad's weeks of convalescence the bond between them had grown very strong. Stunned by this unexpected turn of events, Katy went home and told Jim that she wanted to put Lad back on the trialling circuit.

Jim told Katy that she had one problem – she couldn't whistle. She was, in fact, completely toneless. Lad was trained to two different whistles and if Katy couldn't master these, she would never be able to handle him at a distance. This was indeed a problem. It wasn't as if Katy hadn't tried to teach herself to whistle. Aware of her shortcoming, she had made many efforts to learn in the past and had failed miserably. She had a flat shepherd's whistle, but she had never managed to get a single note out of it. Jim was unsympathetic. 'It's about time you learned,' he told her, 'You go on that there fell and you don't come down until you can whistle properly.' Secretly, Katy was a little scared of her eighteen-stone hulk of a mentor, so she obediently did as she was told. She went up on the fell with Lad, knowing that she dared not go back until she'd got it right. After hours of frustration she managed to get a noise out of the shepherd's whistle and with more practice she succeeded in getting Lad to go right on the right-hand whistle and left on the left-hand one. She returned to the house triumphantly after an absence of twelve hours.

Jim said 'Right then lass, let's watch you,' and Katy nervously demonstrated her new skill. When Lad had collected some sheep and brought them obediently to Katy, Jim turned to her and said, 'Well, that's amazing, Katy, because you're not a very good whistler and that dog must be so clever, because you've changed the tone completely for his left- and right-hand whistles!' It was remarkable that Lad had adapted so quickly to compensate for Katy's lack of musical ability. Inspired by this, she decided to enter him for the next trial.

The following weekend, Jim and Katy both entered for a local trial. Lad and Katy did reasonably well and although they weren't placed, it was clear that the partnership had great potential. A few weeks later, they entered the Garstang Open Championship. There were eighty competitors in total and the course was long and testing, running up a steep hillside. To everyone's amazement, Katy and Lad won it, beating Jim in the process. The judges, she gathered later, hadn't even realized that Lad only had three legs. From that day onwards the other handlers ceased to treat Katy as something of a joke and began to perceive her as a threat. Not only was she a woman, but to top it all, she had beaten them with a three-legged dog. When she realized that they were disgruntled, Katy, unfailingly competitive, became more determined than ever to beat the men at their own game and she and Lad continued to win throughout the summer.

With their mutual pleasure in dogs, trials and each other's company, Jim and Katy enjoyed an idyllic existence. They had the same sense of humour and they enjoyed an excellent social life in the farming community. Katy's original week with Jim had stretched into a year and this year had passed so happily that in 1985 they decided to get married. Jim borrowed a suit from a friend and Katy wore a long white dress over her wellies, but they didn't stay spruced-up for long. As soon as the registry office ceremony was over, they rushed home, changed back into their old jeans and sweaters and shot off to another trial, which, they both agreed, was the perfect way to spend their wedding day.

Shortly after they got married, they moved to Windy Bank Farm near Rawtenstall. Reviewing her victories to date, Katy realized that she and Lad had accumulated enough points to compete at national level. Eagerly, Katy filled in the International Sheepdog Society's forms. However, they replied telling her that she could not compete at this level with a three-legged dog. She was devastated. Her anger and frustration boiled over as she hugged Lad, sobbing her heart out at the injustice of it all. She had worked so hard to qualify and now she would have to start afresh with another dog if she wanted to compete at national level. Some time later, with the gift of hindsight, she realized that the Society had been right and that the tough schedule would have been too much for Lad, but it hurt terribly at the time.

Swallowing her disappointment, Katy began to search for another dog. She eventually bought a large, strikingly good-looking ten-month old puppy called Royal Moss. Moss was full of flair but very hard to handle. His wilful personality mirrored Katy's and consequently, she had to make a conscious effort to be firm but careful in her handling of him. It was good experience for her, as her aptitude for training dogs developed. One day Jim arrived home with a present for Katy – a skinny little four-month old puppy, which he had acquired from a dog dealer. Although she was clearly the runt of the litter, Jim knew her breeder and knew that she had an impeccable bloodline. He warned Katy that if Trim, as she named the puppy, failed to be any good, it would be the trainer's fault not the dog's. To add to her growing kennel, Katy was also given a puppy born to one of Lad's litter sisters, which she named Max.

With four dogs to work, plus trials, plus jobs outdoors on the farm, Katy was working hard. Jim was working hard too and although he and Katy were happy enough when they went off to a trial together, on the home front their relationship was beginning to deteriorate. Katy was no housewife and this caused endless rows. They both drank a great deal and socialized late into the night. Through the day they were therefore tired and jaded, with a tendency to snipe at each another. Sniping turned into full-blown rows and the rows hammered a wedge between them. Katy tried to talk to Jim about their problems, but he refused to discuss them. Desperate to get his attention, Katy started to flirt with other men. This only succeeded in enraging Jim.

Although they were still in love, it became clear that they were making each other increasingly unhappy and with great reluctance, they agreed to part.

Once again, Katy, now aged twenty-six, was on her own, with only her dogs for company. She had no money, so she sold Moss in order to be able to keep herself, Lad, Trim and Max. She hated doing this and bitterly regrets it to this day, as Moss was just beginning to show great promise. In need of a job, Katy headed south and found work in Norfolk, where she was employed to look after five thousand store lambs. It was a complete departure from the type of shepherding she was used to and she hated it. The lambs were reared on root crops and contained within electric fencing, which had to be moved at regular intervals to facilitate strip-grazing. Moving the fences was a muddy, irksome task. The wires were fiddly to shift and they cut into Katy's hands. Despite the voltage running through them, they did not prevent the lambs from escaping and Katy had a tough time trying to keep tabs on her charges. There was no proper work for her dogs and the featureless East Anglian landscape made her yearn for the hills she had left behind. One season was as much as she could take and when an acquaintance from the trialling circuit, Richard Fawcett, offered her a job for the following lambing season on his farm in the Yorkshire Dales, she jumped at it.

Richard and Anne Fawcett have a lovely farm in the heart of Herriot country, near Hardraw in North Yorkshire. Here, where the surrounding land appears to have been crumpled into hills by a giant hand, Katy felt at peace. She loved staying with the Fawcetts and their four children and she threw herself energetically into the lambing season, relishing her surroundings and the chance to use her dogs for the work for which they had been trained. But the six-week lambing season passed all too quickly and after some of the happiest weeks of her life, she was jobless again. She applied for a job further down the dale and was taken on to look after a mixture of sheep and cattle and also to do the milking. It was a live-in position, which rapidly became acutely uncomfortable. Katy worked alongside the farmer all day and this clearly didn't please his wife, who was suspicious of this young, raven-haired girl who spent most of the day in her husband's company. She took to following Katy around like a shadow and in her jealousy she gave her husband a very hard time indeed. There was nothing going on between Katy and her employer, but eventually the atmosphere became intolerable. Katy went to the farmer and explained that she could see how much hassle he was getting. She offered to leave. He was reluctant to lose her – she was a good worker, but he admitted that his family life hadn't been worth living since she arrived, so he let her go.

After a decidedly chequered career, it was at this point in her life that Katy really fell on her feet. Anne Fawcett had just been accepted on a year's art foundation course for mature students at a college in Harrogate. After this, she planned to take a three-year degree course in Hull. This meant that with the exception of weekends, she would be away for the next four years. Katy was offered the job of nanny to the children, as well as the annual lambing contract. In addition, Richard outlined a further scheme which would enable Katy to earn some additional income. 'Why don't you set up a business training sheepdogs for farmers?' he suggested. 'Training dogs is what you're best at and you enjoy it.' With extreme generosity, he offered Katy the use of a field and a barn and told her that she could keep her own small flock of sheep on his ground to use in her training sessions. He added that whenever the children didn't need her, she would be free to devote her time to her dogs and to her new career as a professional trainer.

Although it was some years before Katy really appreciated what a turning point this was in her life, she had the sense at the time to recognize it as a wonderful opportunity. She moved back in with the Fawcetts and placed an advertisement in the *Farmer's Guardian*, offering sheepdog training. That weekend the telephone rang incessantly and by Sunday evening, Katy had a list of over seventy enquiries for her services. It was an auspicious beginning. She selected ten dogs to start with and her new business was underway.

She rapidly realized that she had bitten off more than she could chew. Ten dogs, on top of her own, were quite a handful and although she got through them, in the future she knew better than to take on so many at one time. Farmers tended to send dogs which they had already attempted to train and given up on. They would then pack the dog off to Katy to see what she could do with it. They never gave her any information about what they had already done, or attempted to do with the dog, thus before she could start training, Katy would first need to assess the problems that had occurred through the farmer's bad management. This was much harder than starting from scratch.

Although Katy could train dogs and get them under control in four to five weeks, the minute they returned to their owners, they tended to go back to square one, due to the fact that the owners gave them commands ineptly. A farmer from Skipton returned with a dog which Katy had trained and complained that he couldn't get it to work for him. Katy asked him to show her the problem. He said 'Come bye,' to the dog and it didn't budge. Katy gave the identical command and the dog shot off and collected the sheep. This incident made Katy realize that the people needed training more than the dogs. She applied to the Agricultural Training Board and with their blessing, she became a tutor for farmers as well as their dogs.

She enjoyed her new role as a teacher hugely. Her parents were delighted to hear that she was finally settling down and the relationship between them improved, as Katy and her father joked over the telephone about the similarities between teaching dogs and teaching small boys. To Katy's surprise, she found that many of the people who attended her classes were women. To this day, more women than men come to her with their dogs for training. Katy, comparing her life to theirs, feels sorry for them. 'That's their afternoon off – to come with me for three hours with their sheepdogs. Normally they have to be tied to the kitchen sink looking after the kids, running around after their flaming husbands who just gallivant all over the place doing what they want. I think – the poor things – and I just feel so lucky. Their blooming husbands can't even keep them four sheep so they can practise in a field near the house. Isn't that awful?'

Now that she had time to devote to them, her own dogs were progressing well. Trim had proved to be easily the brightest dog she had ever trained. Katy had shown Trim sheep when she was still a timid, skinny little puppy and she had worked them straight away, clearly demonstrating her natural ability. She won her first nursery trial at the tender age of ten months. Katy was warned by other handlers that she was bringing Trim on too quickly, but Katy knew she would continue to shine.

Max too was coming on a treat. Katy had started his training at the end of her first lambing season with the Fawcetts. Expecting the sort of defiance which she had encountered in Moss, she had cracked down hard on Max right from the outset and he rarely put a foot wrong. He was entered in nursery trials in the winter of 1988 and by the end of the following season, he had won five trials. Katy was understandably smug about this, but she was taken down a few pegs by Richard Fawcett, who was dismayed when he saw Max running the following spring. He observed that Max lacked the confidence to approach his sheep without constantly seeking eye contact with Katy for reassurance. Katy had in fact cracked down on him too hard and although he was unfailingly obedient, he had lost the easy natural style of his early days. Chastened, Katy had to spend the next few months building up Max's confidence, until he would use his initiative once more.

Trim gradually took over prominence from Lad in open trials, as the latter began to show signs of tiredness after completing a long course over difficult terrain. At the end of 1988, Katy decided to retire him from trialling and concentrate on using him within a new facet of her career – giving demonstrations at summer shows. These had come about through Jim, whom Katy inevitably used to bump into at trials. To her delight, they had managed to stay friends and one evening Jim had phoned her to ask if she could stand in for him at a small agricultural show.

Katy found she had a natural flair for demonstrations. She started simply enough, merely showing how her dogs could handle sheep, but after a while, she became more creative. She began to use ducks for her dogs to round up and she acquired her own radio microphone, which enabled her to enliven the performance with an entertaining and spontaneous commentary. Bookings to demonstrate at agricultural shows, game fairs and county shows began to be regular fixtures on her calendar. She was careful to ensure that she never cheapened the work of her dogs by turning her show into a circus act. Nor, after her first season, did she bow to pressure to do more than one show a day, which was too tiring for her animals. Katy's remaining concern was that doing the shows might spoil Max and Trim for trials and shepherding work. She kept a cautious eye on them and in due course she withdrew Max from the demonstration team. She had been using him for brace work – running as a pair with Trim – to demonstrate this skill for the audience, but he was becoming confused. By contrast, Trim had the ability to adapt to her new role without it diminishing her prowess on the trialling field.

In 1989, an official-looking envelope arrived for Katy. It bore an invitation for her to compete in the televised sheepdog trial, *One Man and his Dog*. Katy was ecstatic. For years she had wanted to have a shot at this competition. She had already made the odd television appearance, including a couple of items on *Blue Peter*. She had enjoyed these experiences and when the *One Man and his Dog* film crew turned up at the farm to film her working her dogs, she knew roughly what to expect. This segment of the programme, filmed on the competitor's home ground, is used to introduce them to the viewing audience. The trials themselves are run in heats of three competitors. These heats run over four consecutive weekdays, with the semi-final on the Friday and the final on the Saturday. All the competitors stay on location in hotels, together with the film crew. This year, the trials were to be held at a picturesque location on the edge of Ladybower Reservoir at Derwentwater. Katy's delighted parents decided to spend the week staying locally, so that they could spectate and cheer her on.

Katy was to run Trim. The *One Man and his Dog* competition follows the standard sheepdog trial format – the outrun, when the handler sends the dog away to come round behind the sheep; the lift,

ABOVE Dawn on the Melbury Park Estate in the spring of 1994.

RIGHT August 1962, aged two, with her pet rabbit.

BELOW On a shoot day as a teenager with her father *(sixth from right)*.

ABOVE Judy at Auchlyne, autumn 1993.

LEFT At work on the estate.

ABOVE RIGHT In her Sunday best, checking her beloved Highland Cattle before church.

BELOW RIGHT Judy (*third from right*) with her mother and father (*foreground*) and family, shooting grouse at Auchlyne.

BELOW Judy and Edwina with Sylvia the deer.

ABOVE Mother Mary Agnes inspecting her salted fish, drying in the traditional Shetland manner on the washing line.

LEFT Clothed in the habit of SOLI, in the byre chapel at the Ness.

BELOW LEFT Pat, aged nine (*left*), with her parents and sister Carole at Yarmouth, June 1950.

BELOW RIGHT Pat in service as a nanny, aged seventeen, with the children she used to look after.

ABOVE Lynn fishing on the Wye with her father.

RIGHT In the fishing hut at the Lydbrook Fishery.

BELOW LEFT The young Lynn with a kestrel which she trained with her father.

BELOW RIGHT Already an accomplished angler at the age of eight.

ABOVE Katy receiving the *One Man and his Dog* trophy from the Duchess of Devonshire, in 1989.

BELOW Katy with Jim Cropper at the Royal Lancashire Show 1986, with their dogs (*from left*) Tyne, Royale Moss, Lad, Cap and Fonzi.

ABOVE Katy lambing, in the spring of 1994, on Richard Fawcett's farm near Hardraw in North Yorkshire.

LEFT With Peter Pan, her first pony.

ABOVE Emma on Braco Castle moor during the 1993 grouse hawking season, with pointers Duke and Katy and peregrine falcon Chanel.

LEFT Picking up a falcon from the weathering lawn.

BELOW Aged eight, at Chilham Castle with Wally.

when the dog starts to move the sheep forward; the fetch, when the sheep are brought down the field; the drive, which includes a combination of driving the sheep away from the handler, a cross drive and bringing the sheep to the shedding ring – a circle marked on the ground; the single, when one sheep, marked with a collar, must be separated from the rest of the flock without it going outside the shedding ring; and finally the pen, when all the sheep must be put inside a small pen constructed from four gates. Points, totalling a maximum of 110, are awarded for each section and the competitor must complete the run within an allotted time.

On the morning of her heat, Katy walked to the post trying to control her nerves lest she transmitted them to Trim. The trialling field was tight, leaving no space to get the sheep back under control if they began to run wild. Katy had done her level best to convince herself that she had absolutely no hope of success in the competition, so she should just relax and enjoy it, but with her competitive streak, she was determined that she and Trim should at least make a creditable showing. Their run got off to a good start, with a smooth outrun and lift, and to Katy's pleasure, it continued sweetly. She pushed the gate shut on the penned sheep at the end of the run, knowing that she was in with a chance.

After the conclusion of her two rivals' runs, it was announced that the heat had been won by Katy Cropper and Trim. Katy was walking on air for the next day or so. In her excitement, she didn't think about the semi-final on Friday initially, but as it grew closer, she began to appreciate that the pressure was now on. There are only two competitors in the semi-final and therefore Katy only had one run to beat. She suddenly realized that she was in with a chance of making the final. She began to worry again and there was nothing she could do to quell her nerves. As the time approached for her semi-final run, her nerves worsened and she headed for the post full of misgivings. Sadly, these were not unfounded – by her normal standards, Trim's run was nothing short of atrocious and Katy left the field with a disappointing score of 91 points, certain that she would be easily beaten by her fellow competitor, an Irishman called Paddy Roche.

The luck of the Irish was not apparent that day. Paddy had a decidedly uncooperative bunch of sheep. He started uncomfortably and continued in the same vein, failing completely on the shedding, when the wretched sheep pretended to be superglued together. He lost all ten points for this section, ending with a disappointing score of 88. Katy was through to the final.

Katy fully intended to go to bed early that night to get plenty of sleep, but swept along on the crest of a wave, she ended up joining a rowdy party of handlers for a good supper, plenty to drink and a desperately late night. She fell into bed exhausted in the small hours. When the great day dawned, to her surprise she felt full of beans – she wasn't even nervous. She walked Trim before her run and was relieved to find that she, too, seemed in fine fettle. To Katy's amazement and delight, a huge contingent of her friends from Wensleydale had travelled down to Derwentwater early that morning, to lend their support. Katy was deeply touched and it doubled her commitment to do her best. When the time came, she headed for the post determined to give the other finalist, Willy Cormack, a run for his money.

When the run started, Trim really used her head, keeping the sheep calm as she moved them about the field in an unhurried but precise manner. All the years of effort which Katy had invested in controlling her own volatile, noisy disposition on the trialling field paid dividends in those few minutes as she too remained calm and quiet. The run went like a dream and as the gate swung shut on the pen, she knew she had done her best. All that remained now was to watch Willy's run.

Willy's run was excellent and any hopes that Katy might have had of watching him make a mistake, thereby allowing her to relax, went out of the window. It was all up to the judges and in a state of extreme nervous tension, she waited for the announcement over the loudspeakers. Finally it came through. 'Willy Cormack: 99 points, Katy Cropper: 103 points. The winners of this year's *One Man and his Dog* are Katy Cropper and Trim!' Katy's supporters went wild and Katy, quite overcome, buried her face in Trim's neck and wept unashamedly. So many different emotions overwhelmed her – Trim was truly a dog in a million; Katy had worked so hard for this moment and now at last all the patience and support that her parents and friends had shown towards her over the years, had been rewarded. It was the greatest day of her life. The irony of a woman – the first ever – winning *One Man and his Dog* was not lost on the spectators and on the viewing audience and it was fitting that the trophy was presented by another countrywoman, the Duchess of Devonshire. Katy and Trim returned to Hardraw that evening to drink champagne in the local pub, surrounded by friends and well-wishers.

Winning *One Man and his Dog* broadened Katy's horizons. She gave radio interviews, newspaper interviews and she made many more television appearances, on shows such as *Pebble Mill*, *Kilroy* and *Wogan*. Throughout the latter she felt extremely uncomfortable. She was joined by Lad on cue for the second half of the interview and he helped to reassure her. In the end, she acquitted herself admirably, but she knew that she could have done better. Later, trying to understand why her easy-going confidence had deserted her for that one interview, she realized that she had been thrown by being shown in advance the typed list of questions which Terry Wogan was going to ask her. She had had too much time to think about her responses and consequently on camera, she had tried so hard to remember the answers that she had decided to give, that she had lost her natural spontaneity. This was a lesson learned and she vowed never again to read interview questions beforehand.

To her growing repertoire, Katy also added after-dinner speaking – something which she never prepared for and really enjoyed – and celebrity appearances at events such as Crufts, Olympia and the Smithfield Show. As she charged about the country, going from event to event, she relished the glamorous exposure and the rush of adrenaline which these events brought her. She was even invited to attend the prestigious Women of the Year luncheon. This is an annual event, held at the Savoy Hotel in London. It is not a competition, but a celebration of the achievements of hundreds of women from many different walks of life. Women from the worlds of commerce, politics and government, television and the arts, medicine, engineering and many many more, join together for a noisy and vibrant reception and lunch, to socialize and exchange ideas across a wide spectrum of female achievement. It is a smart occasion, with everyone dressing up to the nines and the guest of honour is often a member of the royal family.

Katy took Trim. There had been no mention of Trim on the invitation, but Katy figured that this was merely an oversight, so she duly presented herself at the door of the River Room at the Savoy, complete with Trim, resplendent in a green bow. 'You can't bring a dog in here!' a smart lady informed her in horrified tones. Katy, lying her head off, said she had phoned the previous week and been given permission to bring Trim. The smart lady capitulated, 'Go and stand in the corner over there and don't let her fight with the guide dogs,' she commanded. Drinking champagne and talking to celebrities a few minutes later, Katy found that she and Trim were the focus of attention from the press. They posed for pictures, then headed down to lunch, where the guest of honour was HRH the Princess of Wales. After it was all over, Katy and Trim, sustained by an excellent lunch of fresh salmon which they had shared, returned to the peace of the Yorkshire Dales. The following morning, they were greeted by their photo in all the newspapers. They had even managed to upstage Diana.

Katy's annual calendar is rich and varied, but there are certain focal points which remain unchanged. Her year starts in April with the lambing. Although she works extremely hard during this six-week period, it is her favourite time of year. She walks for miles and works long hours, but watching the lambing paddocks filling up makes it all worthwhile. This is what her life is all about and this is when a sheepdog can really demonstrate what it has been born and bred to do.

In the beginning of May, the lambs are marked and the ewes with single lambs, which can manage on a sparser quality of pasture than those with twin lambs, are taken up to Dodd Fell, high above the farmhouse. The ewes with twin lambs are kept on better pasture closer to the farm. The shows start during the six-week lambing season, and, heading off for the Devon County Show, Katy hits the road at the start of what will be a long summer season of shows and trials. In recent years, she has been doing more and more shows and fewer trials, but this is a trend she is determined to reverse. Her competitive streak has never lain dormant for long and her enthusiasm for trials now burns as brightly as it ever has.

The trialling season is the same as the show season – May to October, so Katy's diary has to be carefully manipulated to ensure that she can do enough of the big shows to earn her keep, without missing too many of the important trials. The Surrey County Show on May Bank Holiday is followed by the Royal Cornwall in June, and the Royal Show – her favourite – and the Great Yorkshire in July. Katy's early relishing of the shows has inevitably been tempered by the number which she has ended up doing. Although they are financially rewarding, it is arduous spending week after week on the road with a trailer full of animals, all of which must be attended to first at the end of a long hot day. To add to her travelling menagerie, which includes her favourite Swaledale sheep – Fergie, Beatrice and Eugenie – Katy now has a charming Dales pony called Eric. At the start of the show she gallops into the ring on Eric, who then screeches to a halt and stands so still that Katy can drive the sheep right underneath him. She has also developed various props for Lad and his ducks, including a long tunnel and a chute, below which there is a paddling pool which the ducks flop into at the end of the demonstration. Ninety-nine percent of the time, Lad behaves in an exemplary fashion during the demonstrations, but just occasionally he has a brainstorm and much to the amusement of the audiences, he races the ducks through the tunnel, emerging in front of them at the far end, covered in feathers. On hot summer days he will sometimes join the ducks in the paddling pool. This brings the house down.

In trials Katy is still running Max and Trim, who go from strength to strength. Although each trial is important in its own right, the early season open trials earn the winners qualifying points for the English National Sheepdog Trials, which take place during the second or third week of August. One hundred and fifty dogs are entered for this event and it is the second most important trial in the calendar. The highlight of the trialling year, however, is the International Supreme Championship in September, in which the highest scoring dogs of the season compete in national teams. To win the International is undoubtedly the most prestigious accolade in the sheepdog world. In 1990, Katy managed to qualify for the English team with both Max and Trim.

As soon as she knew she'd qualified, Katy worked on her dogs like she'd never worked before. She passionately wanted to win the International and with two dogs, she knew she was in with a chance. The days sped by until September, when, full of pent-up energy and enthusiasm, Katy headed north for the event, which was to be held in Scotland. Unfortunately, the Scottish weather lived up to its dismal reputation and as Katy headed for the peg for her first run with Trim the field was shrouded in thick fog. It was so thick that she couldn't even see the sheep. She was unable to complete the run and Trim was therefore out of the competition. Fortunately, however, by the time her turn came to run Max, conditions had improved and his run got off to an excellent start. It continued well and by the time they got to the pen, Katy knew that they had the highest points in the competition so far. Was this to be their year? At the pen, the sheep became tricky. As she and Max manoeuvred them as carefully as possible, Katy became anxious about time. She was tempted to put the pressure on the sheep to speed things up, but she had to be careful – one false move and she'd blow it. The sheep went in. Just as she was in the process of swinging the gate shut, the hooter sounded the signal for time up and she was eliminated. The energy drained out of her as she and Max left the field. She disappeared from view behind the beer tent, put her face in her hands and wept.

With the ups and downs of the trialling season behind her, Katy hits the road again in October for her annual round of after-dinner speaking. She talks to organizations as diverse as the local cricket club and the Women's Institute – 'They discuss topics such as who is going to make the cherry cake and the blackberry and apple jam for the vicar's party, and I think please God don't let me ever end up like that!' In contrast to this genteel activity, November is tupping time, when the rams are put to the ewes and it is also the month when Katy must start to carry feed up on to Dodd Fell to supplement the grass over the winter.

Occasionally Katy will go away to stay with friends around Christmas time. One year while she was staying with a friend in Oxfordshire, she went out with the local hunt. As her horse jumped the first fence, she hit her nose on its neck and blood started to pour from her nostrils. Covered in blood but unperturbed, she carried on and had an excellent day. In the evening she went to a cocktail party, together with many of the people who had been amongst the field that day. She was making small talk with an extremely educated woman, when the woman said, 'Did you see that poor girl galloping past – blood streaming out of her nose? She was swigging out of her hip flask as she went along!'

'No, I missed her,' Katy replied, highly amused.

On her home turf, Katy hunts regularly with the fell packs which follow hounds on foot over the rocky terrain.

In January and February the ewes are gathered and scanned to see if they are in lamb. The scanner will also reveal whether it is a single lamb or twins. In the winter evenings, Katy indulges her love of drawing – mainly dogs, sheep and ponies. At this time of year she organizes a special sheepdog trial in aid of the Christian Children Fund of Great Britain. In February and March, having fitted in training classes for her local human and canine pupils all the year round, she holds special three-day residential courses which are attended by people from all over the country. The courses are run in conjunction with the nearby Stone House Hotel, for groups of eight people. Katy enjoys teaching these classes as the people who attend them are drawn from a wide range of professions and backgrounds. As her year comes full circle, she starts to look forward once again to the first lambs of the season.

Katy has recently written a book about her life, entitled, *A Dog's*

Life in the Yorkshire Dales. The last line of it reads 'There is nothing in the world which could persuade me to give up the shepherd's life.' Mentally she adds, 'Except a chap with five million quid!' He'd have to be a pretty special chap to take her away from it all though, as Katy has got her priorities straight. As she drives back up the motorway after a show, she turns off at junction 37 to be greeted by the sight of the Howgill Fells stretching out before her and she thinks 'Oh bliss.' The first thing she does when she arrives home is to put on her boots, let her dogs out of the kennel and go for a walk right up on the fell. Here, the peace of these beautiful surroundings seeps into her and her busy schedule is temporarily forgotten. In the evening, if she is not too tired, she may jump on her latest acquisition – an antique Massey Ferguson tractor called Miriam, which cost her three hundred pounds – 'a bargain because she's a petrol one' – and trundle off down to the pub for a quiet drink.

She still wants to win the coveted International Championship. She thinks that her star of the future will be Tess – a puppy who is showing great promise and who, armed with an endearing personality, has managed to inveigle herself out of the kennel and into the beautiful Dales cottage where Katy now lives. Here, Tess stretches out in front of the fire alongside Lad, who is now sporting a coat of distinguished grey hairs and seems set to live to a ripe old age. Joining them by the fire, Katy contemplates her life. She loves living in the Dales, but always the maverick, she also loves the variety in her life which takes her away from them and the excitement of never knowing what lies around the corner.

'I look at the beauty of this place and the freedom of it all and its just fantastic, but then after a while I begin to think, "Oh I want to do something else," so I have a good life because it's a contrast between shepherding, teaching people how to train sheepdogs, training sheepdogs and doing shows. I'm a lucky bugger really . . .'

CHAPTER 4

Mother Mary Agnes

NUN

On first meeting Mother Mary Agnes, one immediately becomes aware of the serenity which she exudes from every pore. She moves gracefully, without a trace of anxiety or urgency and she has a quality of stillness about her which could only stem from inner tranquillity. She clearly has a great sense of fun – she is quick to smile and to see a joke. Small in stature, with rounded, weather-worn features, she has finely etched smile lines, which crinkle from the corners of her eyes and mouth. From her manner and appearance, it is hard to believe that this quiet, unassuming woman has founded an entire religious order and carved out a life for herself and for those who have joined her, on one of the most remote, inhospitable and yet beautiful islands at the northern extremity of the British Isles. Hers is indeed a remarkable story.

Pat Millington was born on the 11 October 1941 to a working-class couple who lived in a small Nottinghamshire mining village. Pat's mother was crippled with polio and she had been advised not to have children, but she so much wanted a family that she took the risk and Pat was joined by a sister, Carole, when she was four. It was a very happy childhood for the two girls. Their parents doted on them and made plenty of time for the family to be together. Despite living in an industrial village, Pat and Carole were country children. After school each day they ran at will in the fields and woods which surrounded their rural hamlet. At weekends, they would climb into the sidecar of their father's motorbike and the family would set off for Skegness and the seaside. These trips imbued Pat with a passion for the sea which has remained with her throughout her life.

From a very tender age, Pat had clear ideas about her future. She wanted to be a lady farm labourer and then eventually to marry a farmer. With this vision clear in her mind, she daydreamed through school and lived for her release from the classroom, when she could be free to explore the countryside and travel once again to the sea. Her introduction to the church came in the form of Sunday school, which she bitterly resented for usurping part of the weekend. She was, however, fascinated by the church itself. Passing by one day, at the age of ten, she plucked up courage to push open the heavy wooden door and venture inside. She crept down the aisle, enjoying the cool sunlight which filtered through the high windows, and knelt to offer a prayer at the altar. After completing her prayer, she turned and ran, out of the door and all the way home, filled with a joy that she had never experienced before.

When Pat was fifteen her best friend, a podgy local farmer's daughter, affectionately known as 'Dump', announced that she was going to attend confirmation classes. Pat, not wanting to be left out, asked her parents if she could attend the classes too. Her parents were, to her surprise, less than keen to give their permission, but after a lengthy discussion, during which Pat argued determinedly, using any ruse she could think of, they capitulated and Pat was allowed to go to the vicarage to join the sessions. It was through these regular visits to the vicarage that Pat inadvertently acquired her first job. The vicar's wife, Mrs Newbury, who had been observing this quiet, helpful girl over the course of her visits, suggested to Pat one day that she might like to become a nanny to the children of some relatives of hers, who lived in a beautiful house at Tibshelf in Derbyshire. She explained that the children's grandfather, Audouin Oakes, who lived nearby, had a house in Chelsea and a castle in Scotland, so the job would include opportunities to travel.

Pat immediately fell in love with the idea, but she knew that her parents would be desperately disappointed because they had always hoped that she would become a teacher. Nevertheless, she went home and told them about the job, waiting anxiously for their reaction. Their response was worse than she had expected, not because they put obstacles in her way, but because they were so deeply upset that she was to go away. However, after they had visited the home of the James family – Pat's potential employers – and Elizabeth James had visited them at their own house, the decision was finalized. At the age of fifteen, Pat severed the last bonds of her childhood, as she parted painfully from her parents and left home to embark on her new career.

Soon after her arrival, Pat realized that she had really fallen on her feet. The house, called the Cedars, was lovely, set in beautiful gardens, and her work with the children gave her ample opportunity to get out into the surrounding countryside. Pushing the youngest in a pram, she would take the children to a nearby farm, where they could lean over the stall doors to see the animals. As she manipulated the heavy pram along muddy farm tracks, they would all delight in watching the lambs playing in the fields. Trips to London were also filled with pleasure for Pat, as she took the children to museums and for walks beside the Serpentine. Being much younger than the other nannies, who paraded around this area with regal dignity, Pat would try to pretend that she wasn't a nanny at all – rather that she was the children's mother, covering for the nanny on her day off. Pulling the collar of her coat high to cover her starched collar and tucking her apron up, she would do her best to perpetuate this myth, although much to her irritation, the impression was spoiled when her apron persistently peeked out below her coat.

The highlight of the year was the annual trip to Skipness Castle. With growing excitement, Pat would board the sleeper to Glasgow, sharing a compartment with Philip, the elder of the two boys. At Glasgow they were met by Audouin Oakes, who transferred them to his Rolls and drove them on the long journey to Skipness. Skipness Castle is set in stunning surroundings, towering majestically over the rugged coastline of the west coast of Scotland. There, Pat's days were filled with sailing, swimming, fishing for mackerel and picnicking with the children, as she delighted in renewing her acquaintance with the sea. During these summer holidays, she fell deeply in love with Scotland and decided that she would like to live there some day.

It was at Skipness that she first met Simon, the younger brother of her employer. Simon was greatly taken with this vivacious young nanny, who sparkled with happiness and good humour. On the evenings when there was Scottish dancing in the village, he ensured that he monopolized Pat, whirling her energetically around the floor until they were both exhausted. Afterwards, he would walk her home, teasing her with tales of ghosts haunting the old castle ruins, which lay alongside the main building. Pat also saw Simon when the James family stayed with Audouin Oakes at his magnificent house, Felley Priory, on the outskirts of Pat's home village. Tobogganing on the drive one day with the children, Pat turned to gaze at the old priory, picturesquely shrouded in its halo of snow and she was suddenly filled with a longing to have been born into such a family – it seemed to offer everything she wanted.

As Pat mused on her future, the days slipped rapidly by until it was time to return to Skipness for the family summer holiday. Simon was again at her side whenever he could be. He taught Pat how to drive a tractor, how to play croquet and billiards and he let her drive his car. The bond between them was clear for all to see. One evening, shortly before her eighteenth birthday, they took a stroll outside. In the moonlight, with the waves lashing the shore beyond them, Simon asked Pat to marry him. To her own surprise, she hesitated. Pleading for time to think, she spent the next few days agonizing over the decision she must make, vacillating as she toyed with her conscience. Simon, in an agony of his own, pressed her for an answer. Finally, she reached a decision. She didn't love Simon and therefore, despite the fact that he was offering a secure future, a home in Scotland and a lifestyle which she'd grown to love, she had to say no.

Back at Tibshelf, Pat fell under the influence of a young Methodist lay preacher and she embarked on a course which would enable her, too, to become a local lay preacher. One of her first sermons, delivered in October 1960, in the four-day interval between her parent's twenty-first wedding anniversary and her nineteenth birthday, was based on the text, 'Weep not; she is not dead, but sleepeth.' Her parent's wedding anniversary had been a happy family occasion – they had been delighted to see Pat and were full of excitement because, together with Carole, they were going to travel the following day to Luton, to stay with Pat's paternal aunt. Here, they were at last going to part company from their ageing motorbike and sidecar and purchase a small car. Plans had been made to return home in the car, to be back in time for Pat's birthday.

Bathing the children at the Cedars on the eve of her birthday, Pat heard the telephone ringing downstairs. Unaccountably, she felt a horrid sense of premonition, as she slipped downstairs to retrieve some small item which she needed. Her fears crystallized as she heard Elizabeth James talking in the next room. 'Oh, how dreadful . . . did you say Kettering? Thank you so much for letting us know.' After a pause which seemed interminable, Elizabeth appeared and with a stricken face, explained to Pat that her family had been involved in a car accident and that her mother had been killed.

In a state of shock, Pat travelled with Audouin Oakes to Kettering the next day – to the hospital where her father and sister were recovering from shock and nursing some bad bruises. She found her father sitting on the side of his bed, wearing an old gabardine raincoat, belted tightly round the middle. He seemed to have shrunk and his face was blotched with crying. Despite her own grief, Pat realized that she would have to take over, to let him lean on her until he recovered sufficiently to care for himself and for the fourteen-year-old Carole. A few days later, walking behind her mother's coffin to the strains of 'The Lord is My Shepherd', Pat was suddenly and joyfully filled with her mother's spirit. She knew that her mother was not in that coffin and that death was not the end – it was merely the door to eternal life.

For the next six months, Pat stayed at home, looking after her father and her sister. During this time, she was supported by the goodwill of friends, including Audouin Oakes and Cyril Miles, the local vicar. During one of many lengthy conversations, Cyril Miles told her about St Francis of Assisi, explaining the growth of the Franciscan Order and the founding of the Tertiary movement. He also told Pat that he considered that she would make a good Franciscan Tertiary. Pat took home a sheaf of papers about the movement and leafed through them, but forgot about them.

If the question of her future was not uppermost in Pat's mind, it certainly was in those of her friends, who eventually felt that her father had recovered sufficiently to allow her to move on. Through an introduction by Audouin Oakes, Pat accepted a job at Greenways – a large country house in Essex, which provided a centre for people in need, ranging from unmarried mothers to maladjusted children. With her easygoing nature and her ability to care for others, Pat fitted in happily to life at the Greenways mission. On her day off her treat was to visit the little cottage which belonged to 'Padre', the Baptist minister who was warden of the mission, who only used it at weekends. Alone, she spent many happy hours exploring the books in Padre's overflowing library. One book in particular gave her food for thought. It was entitled *St Francis in the World Today*. From this slim volume, she learned that St Francis had given away everything that he had and through this act had come to experience perfect joy. Pat realized that St Francis had found what she herself was looking for – the fulfilment which she had failed to find in seeking a husband and family of her own. Deeply influenced by this message, back at Greenways, Pat spent her entire weekly wage packet on the residents at the mission. Awkwardly, she explained to Padre that she wanted to test the Franciscan way of life.

Shortly after this, Audouin Oakes visited her again. He had two purposes in mind – firstly he wanted to find out if Pat's feelings over Simon had changed. As he suspected, they hadn't. Secondly. he wanted to offer her the chance to train as a moral welfare worker, at his expense. Whilst Pat dwelt on this kind offer, he invited her to his house in Chelsea, where she could spend a couple of days in luxury to consider her options. She accepted the invitation and on her arrival, Audouin gave her a book to read, entitled *Religious Communities of the Anglican Communion*. He directed her to the details of a small community of Franciscan women. Amazed by this coincidence, Pat took the book up to her room to read. As she devoured the pages, she could feel a strong sense of destiny beckoning.

Confused, Pat still needed to make a decision about her immediate future. Inspired by her work with unmarried mothers at the mission, she wanted to get to Cambridge to see the matron of a mother and baby home, where she hoped that there might be an opening for her for a working holiday, with a view to undertaking this line of work on a full-time basis. Unfortunately though, she had no money and thus no means of getting to Cambridge. At breakfast next morning, out of the blue, Audouin Oakes casually mentioned that he had to go to Cambridge that day on business and invited Pat to accompany him. Some hours later, after a lengthy wait in the reception room of the mother and baby home, Pat was ushered into the matron's office. Clearly, the matron was a very busy woman and Pat felt guilty about taking up her valuable time, but as they talked, her eye was drawn to a photograph of a nun on the mantelpiece. Suddenly, she found herself blurting out her desire to become a Franciscan Tertiary. To her astonishment, the matron revealed that she, too, had tried her vocation at a little Franciscan community in Devon. 'That's the Reverend Mother,' she told Pat, indicating the photograph, 'would you like me to write to her for you?'

Two months later, Pat joined the community in Devon at the age of twenty-one, having disposed of everything she owned – even her mother's letters, which she valued above all her other possessions. The convent had thirty-six acres of ground, much of which the sisters farmed. Being the youngest in residence, Pat soon undertook a variety of outdoor jobs, all of which she enjoyed immensely. Initially, she had to learn how to handle various implements, such as a hook, an axe and larger items of machinery, like the convent's old-fashioned, heavy rotavator. With enthusiasm, she settled into life within the community and cheerfully threw herself into the round of seasonal tasks, tilling the rich red Devonshire soil, sowing seeds, planting crops and thinning trees in the small woodland plantation. She also mastered the basics of animal husbandry, as she learned to muck out and feed the community's pigs and poultry. The knowledge she gained from doing these jobs was to stand her in good stead in the years which lay ahead.

This country life combined joyously with Pat's progression from postulant to novice, when she received her new name of Agnes, after St Agnes of Assisi. On St David's Day, 1966, Sister Agnes made her temporary vows, with three years to wait before she would make her solemn profession of life vows. In the interim, she suffered only one brief period when she questioned her conviction for the religious way of life. All the sisters were invited to the wedding of a local farmer's daughter. Watching the young couple commit to each other, Sister Agnes was suddenly hit very hard by the realization of what she was giving up. Throughout her young life, she had longed for the day when she would marry and bring up a family of her own in the country. Now she was preparing to dedicate her life to God. For the first time since her arrival in Devon, she felt serious doubt.

In the days that followed, she sought reassurance and encouragement from her superiors. To her dismay, she received little. This questioning was an essential part of the process of self-awareness, which she had to achieve before taking her life vows. After much soul searching, she came through it on her own and on 1 July 1969, at the age of twenty-seven, Sister Agnes pledged herself to Christ.

Amongst the sisters, there were those who had tried their vocation at the community, but had found that they were eventually called to a different cause. Rosemary Thompson, formerly Sister Columba, had discovered that her true vocation was working with handicapped children and she had left the community to become a teacher at a school for the deaf. Whilst she was teaching, she had kept loosely in touch with the convent and eventually, she returned to become a tertiary member, resuming her former name. Attracted by Sister Columba's extroverted nature and good humour, Sister Agnes quickly built up a rapport with her and together they planned a trip to Iona, with the blessing of the Reverend Mother.

Sister Columba paid the fares for both of them and they boarded a train at Exeter on 7 October 1976. As the train sped towards Scotland, Sister Agnes once again felt destiny reaching out to her as she progressed northwards. On arrival in Scotland, they spent the night with friends in Paisley, before catching the boat from Oban to Craignure on the Isle of Mull. From here, they were supposed to catch the inter-island ferry to Iona, but to their dismay, they arrived in time to see the boat returning from its last crossing of the day. The ferryman stubbornly refused to take them across, so they headed miserably into a nearby café for a cup of tea, whilst they considered their predicament. Iona, glistening in the afternoon sun, lay tantalizingly close across the sound.

The owner of the café provided a sympathetic ear whilst they drank their tea and in due course he disappeared, returning with good news. He had telephoned a friend on Iona who had a small boat. Bruce Wall, he informed the sisters, was willing to come over and pick them up. Vastly relieved, they just had time to drink another cup of tea, before returning to the jetty to watch Bruce arrive in a compact and rather unstable-looking craft. As the boat rocked precariously, the sisters and their luggage were lowered over the side and they were soon on their way. As the spray stung her face, Sister Agnes was entranced by the beauty of the sea and by the haunting call of the curlew, which welcomed them as they disembarked. That night, safe in their digs, they were lulled to sleep by the noise of the waves.

Sister Agnes increasingly fell under the spell of the island and the restless tides which beat back and forth on its shores. Returning one evening after a long walk, she went up to bed, but lay awake, listening to the pulsing rhythm of the sea. The beat of it matched the beat of her heart and as she strained her ears to its music, she heard a voice. She listened. There was no mistaking its message. In awe, she slept.

Awakening the next morning, she explored her feelings, rewinding the message in her head. She could not believe it, yet she had been clearly told that she was to bring the religious life back to the islands. Had she understood this correctly, or was Iona getting under her skin – bewitching her? Suddenly reaching a decision, she determined for the first time in her life to put God to the test. She knelt in prayer. 'Please God is it You or is it me? I must know. If it's You, then let the island invite me. Invite me to return. To come back and live here, and let it do so before we leave.'

Feeling better, she went outside to talk to Bruce Wall, who was painting the outside of the house they were staying in, to ask him directions for a walk which she and Sister Columba had planned to St Columba's Bay. Seeing her emerge from the house, Bruce hurried over to her – clearly he had something on his mind. 'Sister,' he began urgently, 'I was thinking of you last night, and I was thinking, why don't you come and live here? . . . You could re-build the nunnery.'

Sister Agnes reeled in astonishment. This was too soon – she had not expected a response so quickly and she was certainly not ready to discuss it with anyone. She laughed off his invitation, although she knew it was heartfelt. Later, as she and Sister Columba walked over to St Columba's Bay, she felt a strange sensation – as if her feet were being drawn down, to take root in the depths of the earth. All too soon, the holiday came to an end and the sisters returned to Devon.

The months which followed were the hardest of Sister Agnes's life. She knew with utter conviction that God was calling her to return to the islands, but she did not know how or when. There was no confusion in her mind, just an agony of waiting for the sign to proceed. The timing had to be right and it was not up to her. The months became years and the years became harder still. During this time, she confided only in her father and he encouraged her, saying that he was sure God was calling her to the islands. Shortly afterwards, he was taken seriously ill and died in hospital. Sister Agnes was comforted by the knowledge that her parents were together once more.

Nearly seven years after the trip to Iona, she was called in to see the Reverend Mother, who informed her that she had received a letter from two retired friends of the community, who rented a small holiday cottage on Fetlar in the Shetland Isles. Knowing how much Sister Agnes had enjoyed her time on Iona, they had written to ask if she would like to join them on Fetlar for a holiday. The answer was an enthusiastic yes and on 7 October 1983, exactly seven years to the day since she began her travels to Iona, Sister Agnes set forth for the Shetlands. A fourteen-hour sea crossing and two smaller ferries later, she arrived at Fetlar's tiny jetty, to a warm welcome from her friends.

One of Sister Agnes's greatest pleasures was to walk and walk, exploring the barren beauty of Fetlar, with its dramatic sea vistas. One walk took her past a little croft house, which was clearly unoccupied and appeared, to judge by the holes in the roof, to be falling into disrepair. She reflected on the sadness of this lovely little house, with its outbuildings and half an acre of ground, becoming increasingly run down. Next door to it, there was another small croft house which bore witness to the fate which seemed likely to befall its neighbour, as it appeared dilapidated beyond repair. Her friends informed her that the croft with the hole in the roof was called the Ness and the one next door, Lower Ness. They both belonged, she was told, to the Cheyne family, who owned another, much larger house which they used for holidays, a short distance down the road.

Sister Agnes purchased some postcards to send south, including one chosen with particular care to send to the chaplain in Devon, which she thought he might appreciate. The remainder of her time on the island passed all too quickly. On the last day, she climbed to the ancient chapel site of Halliara-Kirk. There was a cold wind blowing, and as she clutched her cloak closely around her, she heard again the call from God. The time had come to proceed with her vocation. She could answer no and that would be an end to her calling as it was meant to be, or she could answer yes, take her courage in both hands and forge a route to bring the religious life back to the northern isles. She had been waiting for this second call for seven years. With no idea of how she could do it, her answer was yes.

On her return to Devon, the chaplain met her at Exeter station.

Thanking her for her postcard, he said, 'Coincidentally, it was identical to the one that Sandy Cheyne sent us last year, when he and his wife and son were on Fetlar.' To Sister Agnes's astonishment, she learned that the Cheynes were relatives by marriage to the chaplain's wife. Mulling over this strange coincidence back at the convent, she knew meanwhile that she must face up to higher priorities – it was time to inform the warden of her call and to ask for his blessing to allow her to test her vocation.

To her disappointment, the warden was not able to make his regular quarterly visit to the convent the following month, so Sister Agnes, unable to contain herself for a further three months, decided to put pen to paper. In great detail, she explained her calling on Iona and the agonizing seven years which had followed before her second calling on Fetlar. She further outlined her vision of a group of three or four sisters, living together in a small croft house to form a tiny community, which would live by the ideals of the early Franciscans. Their living would preferably be earned through manual labour. She explained that she knew for sure that it was now a case of 'do or die' and added, 'Only in the knowing of this, and at this point, have I the moral courage to make and pursue this decision, and I request to do so, believing it to be the truth, and asking the Community's blessing.' She handed the letter to the Reverend Mother, for her to read before forwarding it to the warden.

Two weeks of silence followed, torturing her every waking moment. Then at last came the answer she had been waiting for – she was released from her obligations to the Community, though not from her religious vows. At the age of forty-two, Sister Agnes was free and privileged to test a call within a call.

Her first move was to stay with Rosemary, who was by this time aged sixty and living in retirement in Ilfracombe in Devon. Due to nursing her dying father and for various other reasons, Rosemary had left the Community in Devon soon after leaving Iona. One of Sister Agnes's first tasks when she arrived at Rosemary's was to draft a careful letter to the Cheynes, asking if they had a property which they would be prepared to lease to her on Fetlar – the chaplain had supplied their address. In reply, Sandy Cheyne explained that he had only one property which he could lease to her and this was a small croft house called the Ness. She could rent it for the sum of £200 per year. When this reply was received, Rosemary became caught up in the excitement too.

The Community had given Sister Agnes three hundred pounds with which to make a start. With Rosemary's help, she chose some simple furniture for the Ness, spending fifty percent of her funds in the process. The major problem they discovered, was the cost of transporting these items of furniture up to the Shetlands. The cheapest estimate was sixteen hundred pounds – a far cry from the one hundred and fifty pounds which she had left. As time went by, this amount dwindled to one hundred and twenty pounds and she became increasingly anxious. In her anxiety, she turned, as she always did, to God for help. 'I only want what I need,' she prayed, 'no more.' The next day two cheques arrived – one for forty-nine pounds and the other for fifty pounds. They were followed by ten £10 notes, pushed under the door in an envelope, accompanied by an anonymous note which read, 'I thought you could be doing with this.'

Sister Agnes's fears evaporated, as she now knew that she would receive sufficient funds to transport the trappings of her new life north. This knowledge was sealed when a clergyman friend in Somerset sent her a cheque for one thousand pounds. Still a few hundred pounds short of her target, she was drinking tea with friends soon after, when they mentioned that a mutual acquaintance, Derek, had to deliver some furniture to Shetland himself and could possibly take her furniture in one of his vans. Hurrying round to see Derek, Sister Agnes discovered that he had already worked out a most ingenious costing, designed to keep her expenditure to the minimum.

'I will get the older of my two furniture vans MOT-ed and take your stuff to Fetlar in that. Then, to make the trip cheaper, what I plan to do is to leave it on Fetlar with you . . . I was going to sell it anyway, you see, and I won't get more than two or three hundred pounds for it . . . so if you have it, you'll see something for your money, and we'll have the pleasure of a lovely trip.' Derek's wife,

Alison, was apparently keen to accompany him on the adventure north. His final estimate, he told Sister Agnes, was twelve hundred pounds. Although Derek couldn't have known it when he drafted his estimate, this was exactly the amount that she had.

Thus it was that Rosemary, Derek, Alison, Tikki – Rosemary's little dog – and Sister Agnes, complete with a splendid new habit which she had made of oatmeal cloth with a large blue Celtic cross stitched on the front, arrived in Fetlar in late April 1984, after a journey during which she had truly felt herself to be homeward bound. The Ness had been cleaned from top to bottom by friends on the island – Kenny and Mimie and their daughter Anne – and the hole in the roof had been repaired. The few items of furniture were installed and in the six weeks that followed, Rosemary, who was, to Sister Agnes's dismay, initially downcast by the dreary seasonal mists and rain on the island, worked hard with her to turn the little croft house and its environs into a home.

The furniture box was removed from the van and given to Kenny, who used it for storing peat. The truck was sold, yielding enough money for Sister Agnes to live on for the first six months. After Rosemary had returned to Devon, Sister Agnes drew on all her agricultural experience, gleaned from her years working the land in Devon, to enable her to blend her new life as a solitary with the rural tasks which she had to undertake, in order to carve out an existence for herself in Fetlar's remote and beautiful countryside. It was an enormous bonus that at last, too, she could satiate her hunger for the sea.

As she had moved at the end of April, one of the most pressing jobs was to get the garden in order and to sow some crops. This promised to be tricky, as the rough ground at the back of the house had been a field for a great many years. She realized that it would take weeks to transform it, through digging by hand, into a workable patch of ground. She was pondering this depressing prognosis whilst she weeded her front garden one afternoon, when a car drew up. The driver hopped out and introduced himself as Andrew Hughson. He explained that he and his wife crofted the ground surrounding the

Ness and he asked whether she intended to cultivate the ground at the back of the house. On hearing her reply, he immediately offered to plough the ground for her the following week. Whilst making life much easier physically, this was also a mental relief as, with no income, Sister Agnes hoped to grow a surplus of vegetables, so that she could help to support herself by selling some locally. By hand, she would not have been able to get the ground ready in time for the sowing season.

After the ground had been ploughed, she spent many hard hours banging down the ridges with a rake, to get a fine tilth in which to sow the seeds. She then planted potatoes, carrots, onions, peas, radishes, beets, beans and lettuces, fervently hoping that Fetlar would live up to its reputation for being 'the garden of Shetland'. Kenny helped her to erect a small fence around the freshly ploughed half acre, to provide shelter for the crops. Seaweed, she learned, was the best fertilizer available in Shetland and moreover, it was available in abundance for free, if one was prepared to put in the necessary effort to gather it from the shoreline. Armed with a barrow, a fork and a good dose of determination, Sister Agnes, in her working attire of blue corduroy trousers and jumper, blue fisherman's smock and a blue scarf tied tightly around her wimple, would gather heavy loads of seaweed, pushing them laboriously up the steep path from the little inlet closest to the Ness. Frequently her labours were observed with mild curiosity by the seals, which live in the icy cold waters of the North Sea and bask on Shetland's beaches. Seals are naturally nosey and Sister Agnes soon built up an affinity with them and with the other wild creatures which lived in the area. Apart from her two kittens, Skerry and Flugga, they were her only companions during the early months.

The wildlife on Fetlar is varied and spectacular. Otters can frequently be spotted, scurrying among the rocks or frolicking in the waves, turning on their backs to hold fish in their paws while they eat afloat. Sometimes they can be seen down at the jetty, enchanting visitors with their chirruping calls.

For many years, Fetlar was famous for being home to three snowy owls, but unfortunately they were all females, clad in their distinctive plumage of gleaming white feathers, criss-crossed with the black barring which distinguishes them from the males. These beautiful birds were the object of keen interest for the many bird-watchers who make their way to Fetlar each spring and summer. One such amateur ornithologist arrived at the Ness unannounced one day. Drinking a cup of tea with Sister Agnes, he informed her that some other bird-watchers had told him that they had seen some very rare birds on the island, including the nun! The nun was entranced.

Amongst their many attributes, the Shetlands have a wonderful quality of light – lucid and pure. This clarity of light in the day is offset at night, during certain times of the year, by aurora borealis – the northern lights – which illuminate the dark skies with their spectacular son et lumière. Sometimes great shafts of light reach down from the sky directly over the Ness, appearing for all the world to resemble a stairway to heaven. This remarkable sight coincides curiously with Sister Agnes's philosophy on the Ness. The word 'ness' is taken from 'aithness' which means 'the point between'. The Ness is so called because it lies on a point between two headlands, but Sister Agnes thinks of the Ness as the point between heaven and earth.

The early tasks at the Ness were not limited to tidying up the garden and planting crops. The gates were hanging off their hinges and the roofs of the barn and the byre leaked badly and were clearly in urgent need of repair. With her limited resources, Sister Agnes saved up to purchase some hessian and a barrel of tar. Acting on advice received from local people, she set about the onerous task of applying a layer of tar to the roofs, then covering this with a layer of hessian. A roof treated in such a manner has some chance of surviving the gale-force winds which rage back and forth over the Shetlands during the winter months.

Sister Agnes's spiritual director was the Reverend Lewis Shand Smith, the rector of Lerwick on mainland Shetland and the only Anglican priest ministering there. Father Lewis was a kindly man with a wisdom well beyond his years. He would travel periodically to the Ness to join Sister Agnes in prayer and his presence never failed to lift her spirits. He was an excellent advisor, guiding and helping her not just in her religious life, but also with all manner of practical problems. In the worst of the winter weather he braved many a stormy ferry crossing to visit her.

When the gales finally dropped and summer arrived, the crops came up in abundance. Sister Agnes had far more than she could use and realized that if only she had a deep freeze, they could keep her going through the winter. Sadly, such luxuries were well beyond her reach. She tried to put the thought out of her mind, until one day when a friend from Yell, the larger island next door to Fetlar, came over to visit and commented on the quantity of vegetables which Sister Agnes had succeeded in producing. 'Do you have a freezer?' she enquired 'Well, you certainly ought to have one.' She returned home, but phoned later to say that she had acquired a deep freeze. Sister Agnes was horrified, certain that she couldn't afford it, but her friend told her that it was being given to her by a woman who was moving to Fetlar and who asked, in return, to be able to give Sister Agnes a hand in the garden. Sister Agnes was once again touched by the extraordinary kindness of the local people.

In the autumn, Rosemary returned to Fetlar. She admitted to Sister Agnes that she had not wanted to travel to 'the end of the world' one little bit originally, but had had to do so to see Sister Agnes safely moved in. In the intervening months, however, she had found to her surprise that she was dying to get back to Shetland – so much so that she had abandoned her intention to live out her retirement in Ilfracombe and had started negotiations to purchase Lower Ness, next door. She had nearly become a farmer's wife at some stage in her past and although she now felt too old to join Sister Agnes as a sister, she was very attracted to the idea of living alongside the hoped-for community, offering hospitality to visitors and keeping ducks. To Sister Agnes, this was a huge blessing – when Rosemary moved in to Lower Ness, she offered her support in her religious life and invaluable practical back-up in her role as a country woman. Over and above this, the friendship and the encouragement which she offered were appreciated beyond measure.

Sister Agnes had made one of the tiny rooms in the Ness's attic into a little oratory to use as her chapel during the seven daily sessions of prayer. However, shortly after moving in, she went exploring and discovered the door leading to the inside of the cow-byre. Inside, the stone walls were mellowed with age and a wonderful sense of peace pervaded. The old wooden cattle stalls were still standing and the air was heavy with the sweet fragrance of hay. Sister Agnes knew immediately that the byre would make a wonderful chapel – large enough to accommodate not only herself and the family of sisters which she hoped would soon join her, but also a few guests and islanders – should they want to come and join her in prayer and at simple services. She vowed to make a start on its conversion as soon as she had time.

Some months later when a heavy fall of rain prevented her from gardening, she headed into the byre, armed with the only tools she possessed – a small crow bar and a hammer. She had no nails. Firstly, she took down three of the five cattle stalls and using what she could salvage, turned them into rough pews. The roof of the low building was transected by rafters and there were two central roof supports. The one right in the middle posed something of a problem, as although she would have liked to remove it completely, it was clearly load-bearing. With a flash of inspiration, she turned it into a lectern. The second support was further towards the end wall, so she made this into a cross, forming an altar around it. The actual conversion took about three days, and after she had finished, the byre looked as though it had been that way for centuries. Nowadays, during services, with candlelight flickering on the stone walls and animals in the two remaining stalls, it is poignantly reminiscent of the description of the stable in which Christ was born.

The early years at the Ness slipped by. As she followed her daily routine of work and prayer, Sister Agnes dwelt on the founding of the religious order, which she was so certain was her destiny and she decided that when the community was founded, she would like it to be called 'The Society of our Lady of the Isles' – SOLI. To her surprise, however, as the years passed, the anticipated community showed no signs of gathering. People liked to visit her – to come and stay in the caravan parked alongside the Ness, which she had had the good fortune to acquire along the way – but although lots of people wanted to be associated with SOLI in a loose-knit sort of way, nobody asked to join her as a sister. During the first couple of years, she didn't take a break, but Rosemary, ever supportive and watchful, eventually insisted that a small fund should be started, to enable Sister Agnes to go away for a holiday. In due course, and with some reluctance, she headed south, but the break ended up as something of a busman's holiday, as word got out about her travels and she ended up with a string of people to meet and questions to answer. On two occasions she was asked to preach, in venues as far afield as Aberdeen and Cornwall. As she travelled, people got to hear of her story, and many of them urged her to write it down.

Back at the Ness, the thought of writing her story appealed to Sister Agnes. She had always been attracted by any form of creative work and she found herself itching to take up a pen to see if she was capable of putting together a simple autobiography. But, she told herself, it would be very time-consuming. Nevertheless, she decided to consult the Lord, explaining her desire to write, but leaving it up to Him. Later during the same day the post arrived and with it, a letter from an editor at Triangle Books. The editor explained that she had read an article about Sister Agnes in the Church of England Newspaper and wondered if she would be interested in the possibility of a book, telling her story. If so, would she need someone to write it for her, or would she like to try writing it herself? The end result was the publication of A *Tide that Sings* – a beautifully crafted, lyrical book in which Sister Agnes wrote the story of her life, up until the time when she arrived in Fetlar.

The book sold well. Amongst the many spin-offs which resulted from it were the increased number of callers who beat a path to the Ness's door and the escalating number of people who, having been touched by the book, wrote to ask if they could come and stay. Most of these guests wanted both to meet the authoress and to stay in order to rest and recharge their batteries, in an environment where they knew, from the descriptive powers of the book, they could find peace. As the letters came flooding in, Sister Agnes found herself wondering whether there might just be one amongst them which would result in something more important. Now that she had reached so many people, would the book unwittingly become the catalyst for a future sister to join her, so that together they could found the long-awaited community? She was no longer certain that this was what she wanted. After four years as a solitary, she had grown to love her isolated role and had even begun to hope that her original vision had been wrong – perhaps she was supposed to have a solitary vocation? As she later stated, God must have a sense of humour, for no sooner had she begun to believe that she would live out her days happily as a solitary, than He sent her Mary.

It all started with a letter, bearing the familiar phrase, 'Would it be possible for me to spend some time with you on Fetlar?' Mary Lloyd went on to explain that she was a schoolteacher, working in Worcester and that she would like to bring a friend with her – Frances Harwood. Right from the outset, Sister Agnes had a curious feeling about Mary's letter. The dates in July on which Mary and Frances wanted to come were already booked out, so, with some reluctance, she wrote back saying that unfortunately they couldn't come then, but she could squeeze them in in September. Mary's reply stated that those dates were impossible, as she was teaching that week, so she enquired about October. When Sister Agnes explained that, due to the October gales, she could not guarantee that they could get off the island on schedule during that month, plans for the visit broke down and the flow of correspondence dwindled.

In early July, however, Sister Agnes received an unexpected cancellation for the very week which Mary and Frances had originally wanted. She had not been able to put Mary's letters out of her mind, so, recognizing the dates instantly, she wrote and told them about the cancellation, asking them to let her know if they could make it. With a mere four days to get up to Aberdeen, book their passage on the *St Clair* and travel by bus across mainland Shetland to Yell and then to

Fetlar, their plans had to be made precipitously. Despite this, Mary and Frances arrived on Fetlar, on schedule, four days later, highly excited to have reached their destination.

The visit was a great success. Mary's exuberance and chatter contrasted with Frances's quieter manner and both visitors relished the sea air and peaceful surroundings. Sister Agnes really enjoyed their company. Mary, she discovered, as the latter chatted away nineteen to the dozen, had lived in Canada for eighteen years with her doctor husband, but she had been widowed after their return to England the previous year. She was currently hoping to be offered an excellent teaching job back in Canada. At the end of a most enjoyable week, Mary requested a quiet word with Sister Agnes. She explained that Frances had to get back on schedule, but that she could delay her return and she asked very humbly if she might be able to stay on and help out for a further week. 'Make me a work list, a timetable,' she urged, '. . . you know I love cooking and I would do outside jobs such as weeding and painting, as well as happily making cups of tea all day long for as many folk as turned up.'

Sister Agnes had mixed feelings. Observing Mary over the course of the week, she had begun to suspect that her new friend might be experiencing the startings of a call to Fetlar. Suddenly, Sister Agnes was faced with examining her own feelings towards this possibility in depth. She was not at all sure that she could share her idyllic existence with Mary – she would have felt the same way about anyone at that juncture. She turned down the offer of help as gently as she could, but she was not prepared for the reaction. Mary's face was stricken. She obviously minded terribly.

The vision of Mary's face stayed with Sister Agnes during the remainder of the day and by the evening she felt wretchedly guilty at turning down the kind offer of help. She changed her mind and told Mary that she had reconsidered and would love to have her stay on for a further week. Mary was initially delighted, but overnight, fighting with her conscience, she decided that she couldn't really stay – she had other commitments at home which she ought to return to attend to. Consequently, the next morning, she caught the ferry with

Frances, attempting unsuccessfully to hide the tears which flowed freely down her face. Sister Agnes waved good-bye from the dock, feeling very sorry for Mary but rather relieved that she was leaving after all.

During the week that followed, a family of five arrived for their annual break with her, during which they helped out with various chores. Sister Agnes was soon busy organizing them, as they helped her to paint the caravan. Towards the end of the week, she heard the phone ringing. She rushed indoors to answer it, and heard Mary's voice on the other end. 'Have you written that timetable yet?' she enquired, 'Can I come back, please? Next week?' Sister Agnes's heart filled with joy at the prospect and a delighted Mary was told she would be welcome.

The following week flew past as they worked together, finishing off the caravan in the long warm days of summer. While they worked, Sister Agnes outlined her plans for SOLI, explaining that there were already a growing number of people who were associated with the order. She termed these people 'Caim' members, taken from the Celtic word *caim*, meaning 'the circle around'. Tentatively, she enquired whether Mary would like to join her as a Caim member. Mary lost no time in giving her answer and it was a categoric no. She wanted, she explained with vehemence, to join SOLI as a sister.

A heady excitement overtook Sister Agnes – at long last, just when she thought it wasn't meant to be, she had her first aspirant. Her only proviso was that Mary was to wait a year before she moved to Fetlar, to make absolutely certain that she was making the right decision. Mary didn't turn a hair at this stipulation. She continued with her teaching job for the year and visited Sister Agnes whenever she could. Exactly a year to the day, in the summer of 1989, Mary Lloyd arrived on Fetlar to test her vocation.

The intervening year had been mildly frustrating for Sister Agnes. She had tried to buy the Ness, but had been turned down. She was aware that, attached to it as she was, the Ness was extremely small and with Mary's impending arrival, along with Tildy, her little Australian Terrier, space was going to be at a premium. What would

SOLI, taking the official name of Mary Agnes. Against this backdrop of growth and activity, the endless round of rural tasks continued unabated. Although she loves the summer, Mother Agnes relishes the short days of winter, when the brevity of the daylight hours and the gales which rage across the island keep visitors away and she can find a little more space for herself. Despite the inclement weather, there are still outdoor jobs which must be undertaken during the winter. As there are no trees on Fetlar and few on mainland Shetland, the islanders use peat to fuel their open fires. Cutting peat is a skilful task and one which Mother Agnes had to master under the guidance of an islander experienced in the art. The implement used to cut and lift the peat has a long handle, and a right-angled cutting blade and is called a 'tushkar'. Wielded with accuracy, the tushkar enables the user to extract perfect blocks of peat from the rich peat beds which characterize the Shetland terrain.

Outside work during the early months of the year is restricted to urgent repair jobs and to assisting with the tending of the Hughson's sheep – a responsibility which the sisters undertook when the Hughsons moved off the island. Lambing doesn't normally start in Fetlar until May, but on rare occasions, the sisters have known it to start as early as January. If the sheep lamb before the spring grass is through, their diet must be supplemented with sheep nuts and hay. Feeding these offerings to the sheep sounds simple enough, but in reality, it is an exercise fraught with risk. Ideally, it is a two-person job, as an individual approaching the hay store alone tends to get mobbed. This Sister Mary Clare found to her cost. Preoccupied in the Ness one day, Mother Agnes heard a frantic yell from outside. Peering through the window, she was greeted by the spectacle of Sister Mary Clare frantically waving the remains of a bag of sheep nuts, as she sat astride an enormous ewe, amid a sea of other sheep, which were bleating and shoving for all they were worth.

Amongst her many accomplishments, Mother Agnes is now expert at assisting a lambing ewe and rearing orphaned lambs. As a direct result of this latter activity, she and Sister Mary Clare have their own flock of kiddy lambs, which they reared by bottle and which have now become pets. In addition there is Iona, the goat which, despite reservations, Mother Agnes purchased for Sister Mary Clare, who wanted one desperately for a fiftieth birthday present. Iona is a charming animal when one is outside her stall, lending great character to the byre chapel in which she is housed – even the Bishop refers to her as 'the chapel custodian'. However, with the exception of Sister Mary Clare, on whom she clearly dotes, woe betide anyone, including Mother Agnes, who is unfortunate enough to need to enter her stall for the purpose of tending her, for she swiftly turns from angel to monster, butting and generally becoming extremely naughty.

In April, the ground must be rotavated in readiness for the sowing season in May. After the lambing is over, the sheep must be drenched – caught, held and given a dose of medicine to rid them of worms and other internal parasites. As the days lengthen into summer, the visitors start to arrive thick and fast, invited and uninvited, and the sisters' hospitality is stretched to its limits as they battle to find time to do the summer fencing repairs, patch the roofs and generally make the most of the daylight hours. Many of the summer guests volunteer to help with the energetic round of building dry-stone walls, repairs and renewals, but it is still a struggle to keep up as nowadays there always seems to be a vital project in hand which must be got on with in the midst of all the other jobs. On top of arranging the building schedule in 1992, Mother Agnes managed to find the time to write *The Song of the Lark* – a sequel to *A Tide that Sings*.

One of Shetland's greatest assets is the excellence of its fishing. The islanders cash in on this natural resource, not only in commercial terms but also for their own larders. Fishing in the summer is a pleasurable task, but fishing in the winter months is much more difficult, as the waves crash around the coastline and the chill of winter takes its grip. Long before refrigeration was developed, the islanders had to devise a means of preserving fish, enabling them to harvest the seas in the summer in order to sustain themselves through the winter. They learned to salt the fish down and to dry it by taking advantage of the Shetland breeze and pegging it on their washing lines. This quaint but practical habit still exists today and Mother Agnes has been taught how to salt fish in the summer months by her friend Kenny.

Autumn is harvest time, when the crops will be gathered and sorted into neat freezer bags for the winter. The sheep must be drenched again and it is also the time to finish hastily any outdoor work before the onset of winter. As the days draw in and darkness begins to fall as early as two o'clock in the afternoon, the sisters retreat to their roaring peat fire, to answer the hundreds of letters which they receive seasonally coming up to Christmas. This task quite literally takes them the whole of the winter. The rhythm of the seasons echoes the rhythm of the church's year and the highlight of winter is Christmas, when a few of the islanders join the community for Christmas carols in the byre chapel.

The relationship between the community and the islanders has not been without its problems. The funding which the sisters were granted by Shetland Enterprise has been viewed by some islanders as funds taken away from island people under false pretences, by sisters professing to be poor. When Mother Agnes first arrived to live as a solitary, she felt that the islanders respected her, not only for her religious calling but also in her role as a hardworking countrywoman. Now a small but vociferous minority are afraid that the community will take over their island, leaving them feeling suffocated. Although this greatly saddens Mother Agnes, she knows that what she has achieved is of inestimable benefit to those who need the community; they need SOLI for brief but essential sanctuary from the rigours and hardships of their everyday existence and for loving support through correspondence and prayer. Contrary to her detractors' fears, she does not want the community on Fetlar to become much larger, preferring that in the future SOLI should grow through new 'cells' on other islands.

The community now has three properties – the Ness, which they have finally been allowed to purchase, the visitors' centre – 'Tigh Sith' – and Weatherhead, a house on Fetlar where Frances lives, purchased by the community with the proceeds of a gift. They have also been allowed to use Da Gaets, a croft house on the Shetland mainland. Mother Agnes and Sister Mary Clare have now been joined by Sister Mary Aiden and Sybil, an associate, will move to Fetlar in 1994, to share the new house which is planned in phase two of the building plan – Lark's Hame. Although the expansion has latterly been rapid, the community has been developed in harmony with the barren beauty of its island home. Reflecting on this, Mother Agnes is aware of the vital role which the countryside has played in her life – she has tuned herself to its natural rhythm.

'I've always turned to the country for help, if I've needed it – I've turned to it in my joys as well as my sorrows. We are the guardians of a receptacle of great love which is all around us, reflected in the whole of creation, in the island, in the lovely views, in the sea and in the skies. It is easier for people to find love in this place and this is what we seek to give.'

CHAPTER 5

Lynn Woodward

GILLIE

ynn Woodward hooked her first fish at the age of four. She had
been told to strike when she saw the float disappear, and strike
she did, but landing her catch appeared to be more of a
problem. Nobody had told her that once she'd hooked a fish, she'd
have to reel it in. Instead, determined not to lose it, she took a firm
grip on her rod, which had been purchased from Woolworths for fifty
pence, and ran backwards, away from the water's edge. Using all her
strength, she managed to tow the fish right out of the stream and into
the field. Only when she was satisfied that her catch was a safe
distance inland from the bank, did she put her rod down, run over and
pick up her prize. This fish was destined to be the first of many and it
inspired in Lynn a passion for angling which was to shape her future.

Lynn was born on 3 December 1968, in Macclesfield, Cheshire.
At the time, her father was second keeper on the Lower Withington
Estate, but four months later, the family moved to Shropshire, to the
Linley Estate near Bishops Castle, where her father had been offered a
position as a single-handed keeper. The cottage which the family
moved to lay in the rugged terrain of the Welsh borders. From a very
tender age, the young Lynn was totally obsessed with the outdoor life.

The route to this, she could see clearly, was through her father – he was the one who was always outside and therefore, he was the one she wanted to be with. From the age of two, every time her father left the house without her, she burst into tears. Her father, who had always wanted a daughter, was quite willing to take her with him – literally as soon as she was out of nappies – but in taking her along he was faced with something of a practical problem – Lynn was too small to walk and, as a keeper, he had to be mobile. He solved this problem by putting Lynn in a grain sack and carrying her over his shoulder.

Lynn rapidly got used to being left in a variety of strange places. One of these included the corn bin. Her father needed to go and feed the pheasant and although he had taken Lynn with him, he couldn't carry her and the feed for the pheasant on his back at the same time, so he lifted the lid to the corn bin and popped her in, telling her 'Stay there, child – I'll be back.' In due course he returned, to find that Lynn had occupied herself by eating copious amounts of corn, which did her digestive system no good at all. Thereafter, she was left in the Landrover, while her father attended to his daily rounds.

One of the pheasant pens was positioned at the top of a steep slope. Lynn's father parked the Landrover near to it one morning and as usual, left Lynn in the vehicle. He had only walked a few paces from the Landrover when he heard a noise. Turning round, he saw to his horror that Lynn must have taken the hand brake off, for the vehicle had started to roll forward. He leapt towards it and, seizing hold of the bumper, tried ineffectually to hold it back. As it dragged him along he could see that the Landrover was heading straight for the steepest part of the slope and gaining in momentum. He let go of the bumper and ran to the driver's door as the vehicle headed for a fence. Just as he had reached the door and was trying to climb in, the Landrover went through an open gateway and he was knocked back by the gate post.

George Woodward watched horrified as the vehicle careered wildly down the bank. He could see Lynn flailing around inside, screaming every time the Landrover went over a bump. It appeared at one stage to be heading straight for some trees, then mercifully, it swerved and continued on its perilous journey downhill. The angle at which the field dropped away was impossibly steep and every second, he expected to see the vehicle tip over. At the bottom of the slope there was a deeply rutted track, beyond which a brook flowed along the valley floor. As the Landrover headed for the brook at speed, its wheels caught across the ruts and, miraculously, it slowed to a stop, coming to rest in the middle of the brook, some three-quarters of a mile below him.

Incredibly, Lynn was not seriously hurt. She had a few bruises and the experience put her off travelling in the Landrover for a while, but at least she was in one piece. Later on during the same day, George returned to the slope, put the Landrover in a low gear and attempted to drive down the route which the vehicle had followed. He couldn't do it – he had to pull up for fear of the Landrover tipping forward and he came to the conclusion that the only reason the vehicle had stayed upright was the speed at which it had been travelling.

Lynn enjoyed her first years at school. Living in a remote location, she had never had other children to play with. Arriving at school on her first day, she was thrilled to find so many children of her own age. While the other new arrivals were crying as they were separated from their parents, Lynn was loving every minute of it. At the end of the day it was her who was in tears at having to go home. After school, she settled into a routine of arriving home, getting changed and rushing off to find her father.

One of the pheasant release pens was situated a short distance from a stream. Across the stream there were several little plank bridges. While her father was working in the pen one afternoon, Lynn discovered that if she bounced really hard on the plank, she could get quite high. Her father would say to her, 'Don't go bouncing on that bridge or you'll fall in.' But Lynn would wait until he was out of sight and then start bouncing, harder and harder, higher and higher until, one day, she mistimed it. She was coming down as the plank was coming up and hitting it awkwardly, she was chucked into the stream. She landed heavily on the stream bed. Hearing the commotion, her father rushed over, fished her out and added to her extreme discomfort by giving her a clip around the ear for being disobedient. He took her home and dropped her, chastened and sore, into a hot bath. She was blue with bruising for quiet some time.

George Woodward had fished for as long as he could remember. His grandfather had been a tailor and had consequently been able to provide him with a ready supply of bent pins. As a child, he had poached the brooks and ponds around his home in Lancashire and he therefore considered it perfectly normal that Lynn, who he always treated like a boy, should want to fish too. His recollection of the day when she caught her first fish was that he certainly hadn't expected her to catch anything. It was merely a way of keeping her occupied and out of trouble, while he got on with his chores in the pen nearby. 'Sit there and don't move,' he told her, casting her worm and float out into the stream and handing her the rod. He returned to his pheasant, only to be alerted a short time afterwards by a scream. Thinking she'd fallen in again, he ran across the field towards the point where he'd left her, to be greeted by the sight of Lynn running towards him, rod over her shoulder, with about ten feet of line playing out behind her and a half-pound trout flapping across the grass in her wake. Despite the fact that she didn't like fish, she insisted on eating it. After this first experience, Lynn took herself off fishing at regular intervals. She never caught much, but encouraged by her early success and by the fact that she could see the trout in the clear waters of the stream, she never stopped trying.

On shoot days, Lynn was left in the back of her mother's van while her mother 'picked up', or retrieved the shot pheasant with her dogs. Lynn soon got bored with this arrangement and badgered her mother to be allowed to accompany her. The excitement of standing behind the line of guns while a drive was in process quickly palled – Lynn wanted to join the beaters. Unfortunately, at the age of four or five, there was no hope that her little legs could keep going all day in the beating line, as the beaters negotiated the brambles and fallen trees which impeded their path through the woods. Such was her enthusiasm, however, that on subsequent shoot days, two of the beaters grabbed a hand each and literally carried her, suspended between them. As soon as she was big enough to walk unaided, a friend of her father's made her a diminutive made-to-measure thumb stick, about thirty inches in height, to help her when she was beating.

George Woodward was generally hard on Lynn. If she wanted to accompany him on his rounds, she had to toe the line, help out and not whinge about anything. She spent hours sitting in the pheasant pens, observing the birds while her father was working. She got to recognize tell-tale signs that a pheasant was off colour and when she saw one sitting hunched with its feathers fluffed out and its eyes half shut, she'd tell her father with unerring accuracy – 'That's sick.' Her father taught her to kill a pheasant quickly and painlessly by crushing the top of its head between finger and thumb and thereafter she would dispatch sick pheasant without any qualms. She helped with the feeding and when the pheasant chicks were hatching out in the incubators, she spent many hours patiently chipping out chicks which were stuck in their shells.

Her father taught her other lessons, including the identification of all the species of wild birds and animals in the vicinity, both by sight and by their call. Lynn built on these lessons by endlessly studying her comprehensive selection of Ladybird books, depicting the birds and animals of the British Isles. Sometimes in the evenings, her father would take her on his knee and go through the books with her. Despite his gruff attitude towards his young daughter, George grudgingly had to admit that she was a quick learner. When she was only five or six years old, she would frequently go off for long walks by herself, covering several miles and returning with news of all the birds and animals which she had seen. The majority of these reports her father took with a pinch of salt – especially when she informed him on her return one day that she had found a nuthatch nest just down the drive. As it was close to the house, he decided to go and check for himself and to his surprise, he discovered that Lynn, who was only five at the time, was right.

George also taught Lynn how to shoot. Like many children who are exposed to shooting when they are quite young, Lynn desperately wanted to be able to learn to handle a gun herself. The first thing she ever shot was a fox in a snare. She was only four years old at the time, but her father put the .22 rifle to her shoulder and showed her how to look down the barrel and pull the trigger. As soon as she was big enough to use an air gun, she shot a starling and after that, whenever she could, she would go off with the gun on her own.

Despite being country-born and being outside in the fresh air for much of the time, Lynn was not a healthy child. In her first decade, she grew too quickly and, consequently, she outgrew her strength. At her worst, she was quite weak and had to spend long intervals resting. Like all children, she also had her fair share of coughs and colds. On one occasion when she was about five, she had to go to the doctors on her way home from school, to pick up some medicine for a nasty cough. She tried it on her way back to the house and decided that it tasted quite nice. She kept having little sips of the cough mixture and finally she managed to swig down half the bottle. By the time she got home she was feeling very mellow and she decided to go for a walk before going into the house to find her mother. She hadn't got very far from the house before she started to feel rather sleepy.

When Lynn didn't arrive home as normal, her parents were worried. As time went on, they grew more and more anxious and eventually they got together a search party. The search party could find no sign of Lynn. As they didn't even know whether she had in fact returned to the estate, the search was fairly wide-reaching, as they tried to trace her steps from the last time she had been seen. After some hours had passed, everyone was becoming seriously alarmed. Finally, George Woodward decided to search the fields surrounding the house one more time, in case he had missed anything. As he walked down the edge of a field, he heard a faint noise coming from under the hedge. He squatted down and looked, to find Lynn, who had been sound asleep, yawning and stretching. 'Where the bloody hell have you been?' he snapped, hiding his relief as he dragged her to her feet and gave her the customary clip round the ear.

Her father may have been hard on Lynn, but she grew into a polite little girl, who always did her best to come up to the high standards which he set for her. The big house on the Linley Estate was owned by Sir Jasper Moore MP. He was a kindly man and he was very good to Lynn. When his grandchildren came to stay, he would invite her over to the big house to join them. Often he would row them all across the lake to the summerhouse, for a picnic. To her parent's pride, he invariably commented on their return that Lynn's manners were far better than those of his own grandchildren.

In 1976, the family moved south to the Courtfield Estate near Ross-on-Wye in Gloucestershire. George had wanted to go north to get a job in Scotland, but positions for gamekeepers in Scotland invariably seemed to go to Scotsmen. 'I don't think they've forgiven us for Culloden yet,' he commented on the subject. The Courtfield Estate is owned by Patrick Vaughan. He let the shooting to a syndicate run by Andrew Compton, who employed George as a single-handed keeper. The estate also owns Lydbrook Fishery – an attractive double-bank fishery which nestles at the foot of the estate on the River Wye. With his enthusiasm for fishing, George naturally gravitated towards the river and he soon got to know the two professional gillies, whose job it was to accompany fishing clients. When the gillies realized that George was a skilled fisherman, they allowed him to help out. Whenever they were busy and whenever his schedule would permit, George used to take clients out on the river himself. The gillie's real perk is that he gets to fish too. Each client has two fishing rods set up in the boat at the same time. He fishes one and the other one is fished throughout the day on his behalf by the gillie. Thus on the Wye, where the clients were hoping to catch salmon, the gillies were privileged to fish in water where at good times of the year, the fishing sold at a premium.

Lynn, who was eight when the family moved to Gloucestershire, was very drawn by the river. At the time, she wasn't at all interested in salmon fishing – it seemed to her like a lot of effort – but she used to fish enthusiastically for pike and eel. She spent a great deal of time down there and all the regular clients at the fishery got to know her. They would regularly give her fifty pence or some sweets. Lynn particularly enjoyed the company of old Jack, the second gillie. On cold winter days, the gillies would frequently have a nip of something to keep out the chill. Looking for Lynn one day, her father found her sitting in the office in the fishing hut with Jack, drinking sherry. He could immediately see that Lynn had consumed far too much. 'She's only had a little nip,' old Jack assured him. In fact, Lynn had been having little nips all afternoon and was high as a kite. Her mother was not at all impressed when a very giggly Lynn was taken home.

In 1982, when Lynn was fourteen, old Jack retired and a vacancy for a full-time gillie came up. At the same time, the shooting syndicate for which George Woodward was keeper folded and the shooting was let on a much smaller scale to another client. George arranged to do some simple part-time keepering, which he could share with Lynn's mother, but as he would not be fully occupied doing this, he also applied for the position as gillie. As he was by this stage knowledgeable about the fishery and reasonably experienced in taking out clients, he was given the job. The company who leased the fishery – Guest, Keene and Nettlefold – arranged to pay Courtfield Estate rent for a house for the family, with the result that they moved a short distance to a larger cottage. Every day after school, Lynn – whose passion for fishing continued to grow – would rush home, get changed and hurtle down the steep hill to the fishery to see how they had got on that day.

Lynn went to school in the nearby village of Goodrich. Initially, she took her studies quite seriously. She was far from academic, but she knew her father expected her to do well. She went through phases of variously wanting to be a vet, then a forensic scientist, then a policewoman. As time went on, though, she ceased to try as hard as she could, as gradually she became disillusioned with school. Disillusionment hardened into hatred. Everyday school stood between her and the great outdoors. This she bitterly resented – life was too short to waste imprisoned in a classroom. She lived for anything to do with natural history and the countryside and the only subjects she ended up really taking an interest in were art and pottery – and only in those if they depicted animals or birds. Above all else, when she left school she knew that she wanted the country way of life. For this, she figured, she didn't need qualifications, so why bother?

Living in the country, Lynn's social life when she was a teenager consisted mainly of youth-club discos. When she was fifteen, her parents gave her a motorbike. Although she wasn't old enough to ride this on the road, she could ride it around the private roads of the estate. Several older lads from the village who had their own bikes would join her and they would entertain themselves tearing around the estate and having a crafty smoke. Lynn had started smoking when she was fourteen. Her father, who also smoked, occasionally found cigarettes secreted around the house. 'Whose are these?' he would demand. 'They belong to so and so down the road,' Lynn would reply quickly. 'Well, she won't be needing these then,' her father would say, pocketing the cigarettes. Lynn got caught smoking at school one day. Her mother was told, but together they managed to keep the information from her father, who would have been furious.

When she was rising sixteen and rapidly approaching the earliest age at which she could leave school, Lynn realized that she needed to come to a decision about her future. Although she really didn't think she could tolerate an indoor job, there weren't many types of outdoor employment open to a sixteen-year-old girl. Then, just as she was about to leave school, Bill, the other gillie who worked with her father, left. To Lynn, this seemed to be the stroke of good fortune she had been looking for. She immediately said to her father, who by this time was head gillie, that she'd like to take the job. 'What do you bloody mean?' he replied, 'Don't be so daft – you wouldn't make a full-time gillie!' Lynn was bitterly disappointed and extremely upset that her father didn't think she would be up to gillieing – having always been her father's girl and helping him with outdoor work throughout her childhood, she thought that she had proved she was pretty tough. However, her father was unrelenting and the vacancy went to a local man. Lynn was given the choice of either getting herself a job and earning some money, or staying on in the sixth form at school. In the end, she did both – she stayed on at school, where she took 'A' levels in art and pottery and she also got herself a part-time job as a nanny-cum-cook in the big house on the estate.

When she left school at the age of eighteen, Lynn became self-employed. She continued with the nannying and the cooking at weekends, which she enjoyed and in due course, she took another part-time job, helping a farmer with lambing in the winter and harvesting in the summer. This work suited Lynn, but it was tough, especially in the summer time when she found herself hauling bales of straw and hay. The farmer made what were termed 'farmer's bales' which were particularly heavy, so Lynn began to develop a considerable set of muscles. These jobs didn't pay a great deal, so eventually she had to find other work. Unable to find an outdoor job, she had little choice but to take a position in a local factory. The factory made wooden shields for displaying the mounted heads of deer and other trophies. Lynn started work at 7.30 a.m. and her job was to sand these plaques. She detested it. Shut inside all day, she lived for the moment at the end of the afternoon when she was free once more to go for a walk with a gun or pop down to the river. As the months went by, she became more and more unhappy with the job, but she had to earn her keep and she really didn't have an alternative.

Just when she was beginning to despair of ever getting out of the factory, her father came home one evening and announced that the other full-time gillie at the fishery was leaving. This time Lynn stayed quiet. She thought about the job seriously for a few days – by this time she was nineteen and she knew what she wanted. She had always felt that her father would have preferred a son. Consequently, in an effort to please him, she'd acted like a boy throughout her childhood. In some strange way she felt that she had earned the right to apply for a career in a male-dominated profession. She had already lost one chance to work as a gillie and she certainly didn't want to lose another. She discussed it with friends who were gillies on neighbouring beats. They all advised her to go for it. Finally, she broached the subject with her father.

Again, he opposed her. Deep down, her father didn't believe that Lynn really appreciated how tough the life of a gillie could be. Despite the fact that Lynn was older now, that she was seriously keen on her fishing and that she was good at it, he just didn't think gillieing was suitable work for a woman. He tried repeatedly to dissuade her, but eventually Lynn's mother waded in on her behalf, saying, 'Go on George, let her have a go – there's no harm in trying.' Finally, her father gave way.

'I'm having nothing to do with it at all. If you want a job, you write a letter to the owner of the fishery and apply like everyone else. If he wants to see you, go for the interview, but there'll probably be other people and they'll all be men, so you are at a disadvantage already.'

Lynn wrote to the owner of the fishery, the aptly named Mr Plaice, and she received a reply within a couple of days, arranging to meet her. When they met – in a room full of men – he enquired whether she was afraid of worms. Lynn replied that she definitely wasn't – 'In fact,' she added, 'I'm not frightened of many things.' Mr Plaice seemed pleased by this response – he didn't really seem to want to interview her properly at all. He did ask her father if he thought he could work with Lynn, but her father still refused to have anything to do with the decision, saying that Mr Plaice must make up his own mind. Mr Plaice did and not long after he phoned Lynn up. 'Do you really want the job?' he asked her. 'I'd love it,' she replied anxiously. 'Well,' he said, 'when do you want to start?'

Lynn started at a difficult time. It was right at the end of January, just a couple of days before the fishing season opened. She had to be ready to start with clients right from the outset and it was essential that she appeared to be sufficiently professional and proficient. All the fishing at Lydbrook is done from distinctive flat-bottomed boats, known as Wye punts. The boats are equipped with motors, but these are not used for much of the time, for fear of disturbing the fish. One of the jobs of the gillie, therefore, is to row the clients up and down the river between the good pools where they are likely to catch fish. Rowing a boat on a pond or lake is a relatively straightforward technique, but rowing a boat on a river, with a fast-flowing current is an art form. When the river is in spate and the water-level is high, the rowing is a hazardous operation, requiring skill and strength in equal measure. The exertion on the part of the oarsman is extreme – it is difficult even to get the boat moving. To keep disturbance to the salmon to a minimum, the boat must be kept close to the bank. As the current constantly tries to pull the boat into the middle of the river, the gillie must combat this by rowing with one oar, to maintain position. This skill is tricky to perfect.

Lynn had been rowing since she was twelve. At that age she could row fifty yards upstream and fifty yards downstream, but if someone had asked her to row across from one bank to the other, she would probably have ended up 100 yards downstream. The trick in crossing a current is to get the boat at a forty-five degree angle across the river and glide across. If you get the angle wrong, you get swept off downstream. Lynn had worked away at her rowing over the years, and she was reasonably competent, but she had one problem. The fishery is bisected by an old iron bridge, with supports rising out of the water. Lynn had never rowed under it before. As a priority before starting with clients, she had to master the negotiation of this bridge.

George Woodward took Lynn up to the bridge to practise. With great patience, he instructed her – 'Pull the right oar a bit, now pull the left one . . . now let it glide.' Lynn struggled. She tried again. It was very difficult. She had several more abortive attempts. After about an hour of Lynn struggling and failing to master the technique of passing between the bridge supports, her father's patience was beginning to wear a little thin. Finally, he lost his temper. 'Bugger you, you're useless!' he yelled at her. Lynn was upset. She was trying her best and she just couldn't get it right, but she was determined not to be beaten by a stupid bridge. Her father left her to it and she didn't return home until late that evening, after she'd got it right and indeed, could get it right at every attempt.

The dictionary definition of a gillie is 'a man or boy attending sportsmen'. It is therefore hardly surprising that when the season opened a couple of days later, the clients at the Lydbrook Fishery were a little shocked at first to find that their mentor for the day was to be a teenage girl. When they approached her and said 'Where's the gillie?' Lynn would respond 'I'm here, sir.' A look of alarm would cross their faces. 'Well, the river's quite high – do you think you'll be able to row the boat?' Inwardly, Lynn thought 'Well, I'm not going to put up with that sort of attitude,' but outwardly, she would smile reassuringly and say, 'Oh yes, sir, that won't be a problem.'

Lynn's first client was an elderly man, who was an experienced fisherman. Lynn watched the guests arrive that morning with some trepidation. When the time came to set off in the boat, she was acutely aware of the fact that her very first job would be to negotiate the dreaded bridge. Probably due to the fact that she was nervous, she messed it up the first time and got swept back to where they had started. Panic began to mount, but she attempted it again and much to her relief, she managed it at the second attempt. Rowing under the bridge wasn't the only thing she had been practising intensively. At the start of the season, the salmon tend to be comparatively large and it is risky to land one with a net, in case the hook catches in the net and the sheer weight of the fish causes the hook to rip right out of the its mouth. From a boat, the fish can't be beached, so the alternative is to use a 'tailer'. A tailer is a noose, attached to a short pole. The gillie's job is to direct the client to bring the fish alongside the boat and hold it in the upright position, enabling the gillie to slip the noose over the fish and snatch it out of the water as the noose tightens around the tail. It is very much hit or miss. Lynn had never used a tailer before, so her father had made her practise for hours and hours with a piece of wood, carved to the shape of a fish, suspended on a line. She felt a little silly practising with her lump of wood, but the fear of losing a fish for a client was a powerful motivator and she worked away with the tailer until she'd mastered it.

Sadly, Lynn needn't have worried about her proficiency with a tailer on her first day. In fact she didn't have to worry about her proficiency with a tailer that season, because she didn't catch a fish, either on her own or with a client until May, by which time she was using a net. In the intervening months, she had become more and more worried. Her father had caught his first fish with a client on 11 February. As the days wore on through March and April, Lynn began to sweat about her lack of success. Was she positioning the boat badly? Was her fishing simply not up to it? Finally, she was fishing with Mrs

Plaice in May when she managed to hook one. She handed the rod over to the boss's wife and with great relief, succeeded in landing a nice fish. Back at the fishing hut, many photographs were taken and that evening Lynn and her parents celebrated the consummation of her career as a gillie.

The fishing was sold on the basis of a rod on a certain day of the week throughout the whole season. Thus the clients saw Lynn on a weekly basis and gradually, their confidence in her grew. Lynn's real pleasure in the job came from seeing the delight on a client's face when he caught a fish – particularly if it was his first one ever. Being a woman incarcerated in a boat with a man for hours at a time did, however, have its disadvantages for both sides. If a fisherman in her father's boat wanted to take a pee, he simply did it over the side, but the vast majority of men were too embarrassed to do this in the company of a female gillie. Instead, they would either wait cross-legged until the end of the session, or they would request an urgent pit stop at the nearest bank. The odd one was unconcerned and went ahead straight from the boat and this really didn't bother Lynn at all – at least it didn't interrupt the fishing. For Lynn herself, it was much more awkward and she would have to wait until they were fishing the pool opposite the fishing hut, so that she could nip inside.

The responsibilities of a gillie include maintaining the river banks, removing rubbish, clearing debris and obstructions from the water – such as fallen trees – controlling predators like pike and mink and patrolling for poachers. Over and above this, the most important job for a gillie is to assist the fishing clients to the best of his – or her – ability. To do the latter competently, the gillie has to know the stretch of water intimately, what the river bed is like at the best spots, as well as knowing which bait is most likely to attract a fish and how to vary the techniques to suit the weather conditions, the height of the water and the time of year. Of the two-and-three-quarter-mile extent of the Lydbrook Fishery, approximately only a mile in total, consisting of the deepest pools and various special spots scattered along the length of the beat, is actually fished. Every time a fish is caught, it is the responsibility of the gillie to note mentally the exact spot, what sort of day it was, what height the river was and what colour the water was. When the conditions are duplicated, the chances are that there will be another fish in exactly the same place. Thus gillieing is as much a science as it is an art and without the benefit of the gillie's expert knowledge of the river, a client would be most unlikely to catch a fish.

Although Lynn occasionally took two clients in her boat, she avoided this if at all possible, as the weight of the extra person made it exceedingly hard to row. Normally, therefore, it would be just her and the client, each fishing a rod. The gillie is officially fishing the second rod for the client, so if she hooked a fish, it was Lynn's job to alert the client and hand over the rod so that he could land, or attempt to land the salmon and count it as his. The client fishes a pool first and the gillie fishes behind him, covering the water for a second time. Generally, both rods would be baited according to Lynn's judgement. When the water was dark and murky, Lynn would recommend a Devon minnow (a small wooden 'fish') painted in bright colours – red and yellow or green and yellow. When it was clear she would suggest one painted in black and gold or brown and gold. Occasionally, however, a client would go against her advice and make a ridiculous decision about what bait he should use. Fishing the second rod, Lynn would bait it as she thought fit and would often have the satisfaction of hooking a fish while, predictably, the client didn't have an offer all day.

Two people in a boat need to move carefully to keep it stable, as on the water every movement is exaggerated. The rule is that only one person should move at a time. Lynn found that newcomers to boats were very wobbly indeed. Complete beginners could be somewhat hazardous. She always wore a cap and on one occasion, this was jerked sharply off her head by a toby. A toby is a thin sheet of metal, shaped like a small fish, garnished with a treble hook. The client had back cast extremely carelessly and had hooked Lynn's cap, yanking it off her head. Had the toby caught in her face instead of her hat, the client would have ripped the hooks right out of whatever flesh they had been embedded in. Lynn was so stunned by her narrow escape that it took her a few moments to recover her senses and complain. To help her assert her authority in the boat, she rapidly discovered that by calling the clients 'Sir' or 'Madam' she could, if necessary, give them a telling off more easily than if she was on first-name terms.

Some of the clients were clearly exceedingly wealthy. They would pull up outside the fishing hut in Range Rovers and Rolls Royces, kitted out like mobile tackle shops. Sometimes, the impression of suave expertise was spoiled when a client clearly didn't know how to put his rod together. Lynn had to put him right with great tact, to save him from looking like an idiot. Some of the clients would start to talk straight away – 'I've been fishing on the Tay and we caught forty fish and I went fishing on the Test and we caught three fish . . .' Irrespective of their boasting, Lynn could normally tell within five minutes of being in the boat whether they stood any chance of catching a fish that day.

'You get these people – they're multi-multi-millionaires – made millions, possibly billions for their companies. You put a fishing rod in their hands and their brains go straight out of their backsides. People like that, however long they try to fish, there's no hope, because they'll do it right one week then seven days later they've totally forgotten everything you've told them.' Whatever the clients were like when they first arrived, Lynn found that once they were in the boat, she could generally build up a good rapport with them. Fishing is a great leveller. With a salmon on their line, no matter who they were or how experienced as fisherman they were, they would always be reduced to a state of obvious and acute vulnerability.

The excitement of catching a salmon – the king of the river – lies in the playing of the fish. Salmon, whatever their size, embody power and they will put up a good fight. In the first five minutes after hooking one, the fisherman basically has to let the fish do what it wants to do. These are tense moments, as the fisherman tries to work out how big it is and whether he has hooked it sufficiently well to be able to land it. After a while, the angler needs to exert his authority by putting just the right amount of strain on the line to begin to control the fish's movements. It may start to come towards the boat, then decide that it wants to go back out to sea and make a run for it. If the fisherman puts too much strain on the line, he risks ripping out the hooks or 'breaking in the fish' – breaking the line. He needs to feel the fish tire and begin to bring it in, closer and closer, until it lies on its side and the gillie can slip a net under it and lift it victoriously from the water.

As Lynn grew more proficient, the clients would sometimes go up to her father at the end of the day and pat him on the back, saying 'She's done well today.' A little bit of praise was always greatly appreciated. Ever since he had been head gillie, George Woodward had managed to catch the first fish of the season. One year, however, Lynn beat him to it and it was a hell of a good fish too, weighing in at sixteen pounds. Mr Plaice had left a bottle of champagne for the person who caught the first fish of the season. A jubilant Lynn figured that he hadn't said it was strictly for a client, so she had the bottle open the second she got back to the fishing hut before anyone tried to stop her.

The Lydbrook Fishery is a most attractive beat of the Wye. Lynn found that with her knowledge of the countryside, she could enhance the overall experience for the client by pointing out the rich and varied wildlife which lived in the area. She could always spot something to show them – a kingfisher or a dipper or perhaps one of the peregrines which nest nearby at Symond's Yat. The clients appreciated this and it helped to while away the hours if the fishing was unproductive.

Occasionally, Lynn would spot a mink from the boat. Mink are highly destructive if they are left to prey unhindered on a stretch of river. Part of the gillie's job was to control the mink numbers, to protect wildlife on the banks and salmon parr – the young salmon. This was generally done by setting cage traps for the mink on the banks. On one occasion, not long after she'd started work on the river, Lynn spotted a mother and three baby mink. Thinking of the damage this family could do, she rowed across to them and managed to hit one of the babies with a oar. It fell into the water, so she picked it up and put it into the boat. The rest of the mink family beat a hasty retreat.

The young mink in the boat didn't appear to be badly hurt. Looking at it – a little black fat thing about six inches in length – Lynn decided it would make an interesting pet. She showed it to her father. 'You don't want to bloody keep that,' he told her, 'It'll turn nasty.' Undeterred, Lynn took the mink home and showed it to her mother, who was equally unenthusiastic about the prospect of having a mink lodging in her back garden, claiming it would get out and eat her chickens. But Lynn persisted in her defence of the mink and eventually she got her own way. The mink was installed in a stout cage in the garden. It was a male or hob mink and it started to grow rapidly. It grew and grew, until it was nearly two feet in length. By this stage it was consuming an entire rabbit a day. It never bit Lynn, but it was not the most sociable creature and nobody else would go anywhere near it. Returning from the river one evening, Lynn went out to its cage to feed it. The cage was empty. This was no joke – a fully adult hob mink is a formidable creature, armed with a lethal bite. In fear and trepidation, Lynn went in and broke the bad news to her parents. Her mother went berserk, 'It'll eat the dogs!' Lynn retreated to look for it. She searched high and low, but there was no sign. She anxiously checked the chicken run, the garden and the kennels. It was nowhere to be seen. She sincerely hoped it would make itself scarce – if it started on the chickens she would be in serious trouble. Just as she was about to look further afield, she saw a black nose appear from under the shed behind the cage. She rushed inside and told her father. A grim expression came over his face and he grabbed his rifle and followed her out. They watched the gap under the shed intently and sure enough, the mink stuck its head out. It was the last move it ever made.

Mink are not generally scared of people – some fishermen have even been attacked on the river by mink. Lynn was fishing with her boss one afternoon when they saw a mink on the opposite bank. Her boss decided to squeak at it to see if he could get it to come closer. As he squeaked away, attempting to imitate the noise made by a rabbit in trouble, the mink, rather to their surprise, entered the water and began to swim towards them. It must have been really hungry because it came closer and closer to the boat, which was positioned right against the far bank. To their utter amazement, it climbed out of the water, on to the bank and jumped right into the boat. For a few seconds all three stared at each other transfixed until the mink, realizing its mistake, ran off.

Although Lynn loved gillieing it was hard work, particularly when the weather was bad. She really loathed days when it poured with rain and in cold weather, exposed to the elements for protracted lengths of time, she would get chilblains, not just on her fingers and toes, but also on her face and even on her ears. Sometimes the water conditions were totally wrong for fishing and she knew for sure that it was a complete waste of time trying. Other days it just felt dead and the hours crawled past until the end of the day. Sometimes, however, even when conditions weren't perfect, she unaccountably felt optimistic. 'After a while you get to know the water so well that you tend to develop a sixth sense. Sometimes this sixth sense comes along and you just know you're going to catch a fish.'

Off the river, Lynn had little time for a social life. Occasionally, she would see a couple of girlfriends from her school days, but she didn't have a lot in common with them. They simply didn't understand what she did or why she had chosen that way of life. As a result, they had never had much to talk about. 'They'd ask me what I'd been doing and I'd say fishing, and that kind of killed the conversation. One of them has known me for a long time and she thinks I'm a bit of a wild one – a bit heartless because of the shooting and fishing. To talk about the things that other girls or young ladies talk about can be quite awkward for me.' Some women were quite touchy about the length of time she spent in close proximity with their men.

Lynn generally got on much better with men than women. She had various boyfriends in her teens, the most serious of which was a gamekeeper called Shane, whom she met while she was in the sixth form at school. Lynn liked the look of him and rather boldly sent him a letter, asking him out for a drink. He phoned her up and that was the start of a relationship which lasted for three years. After school,

Lynn would get dropped off at the nearby Bishopswood Estate where Shane was under keeper. She would take old clothes to change into and the two of them would spend the evening together before he dropped her back home.

They had a lot in common – they both enjoyed shooting and anything to do with the country, although Shane was not a fisherman. Shane's mother was instrumental in helping Lynn to get her hated job in the factory when she left school. Outside work hours, Shane and Lynn spent as much time together as possible and in due course they announced their engagement. Shortly afterwards, Lynn started work on the river. This put a strain on the relationship. Lynn's father demanded long hours and gave her little or no time off and consequently, Lynn had less time for Shane. Shane hated her working at the fishery and complained about it vociferously. Not long after she started work, he was offered a job in the Cotswolds and announced to Lynn that he was leaving, asking her to go with him. When Lynn had accepted the gillie's job, Mr Plaice had asked her to stay for a minimum of four years. She had agreed – thinking that four years would pass in no time. Now she faced a dilemma. Her fiancé was leaving and wanted her to go with him, but she couldn't let Mr Plaice down and really, she didn't want to. She was thoroughly enjoying her work. She told Shane that she couldn't move, but that she would visit him whenever she could – she had recently passed her driving test at the first attempt.

True to her word, she purchased her first car – a Mark 1 Escort in red with a white roof. She was tremendously proud of this car and whenever her father let her take an afternoon off, she would drive the forty-odd miles to the Cotswolds to visit Shane. George Woodward refused to allow his young daughter to spend the night away, so she had to return late the same evening. Eventually, the geographical difficulties of maintaining the relationship took their toll and with much regret on both sides, the engagement was broken off.

The head keeper on the Bishopswood Estate, where Shane had worked, was called Huw. Even while she had been with Shane, Lynn had always fancied Huw on the quiet – he was eight years older than she was and compared to Shane, he seemed very mature. He left the area and went to Scotland to work for a while, but he eventually returned to Bishopswood and resumed his former position of head keeper. He used to visit George Woodward occasionally and eventually he asked Lynn out. Because of their shared love of the country and country pursuits – including fishing – they were very happy in each other's company and soon fell in love. Seven months later they got engaged and a couple of months after that, Lynn got her parent's permission to move to the Bishopswood Estate, to move in with Huw. They have been together ever since and intend to get married just as soon as they have enough money. They work hard to supplement their income by shooting rabbits at night with a lamp and they don't spend extravagantly on material goods or clothes. Lynn tends to live in baggy trousers and sloppy sweaters – 'I do have a dress – you have to make an effort, you can't go around looking like a hillbilly all the time.' However, saving is not their strong point and if they do get any money together, they tend to spend it on sporting holidays, particularly in Scotland, so that they can indulge their love of stalking deer. They don't spend as much time together as they would like, but basically they are happy and very well suited.

'The strength in our relationship must come through the love of the outdoors. I love my fishing, he loves my fishing. I love his keepering, he loves his keepering and we both enjoy stalking. Every single one of the deer I've shot, he's always been there, so we make a good team.'

The year of a gillie on the Wye starts on 26 January, when the season opens for salmon fishing. Sometimes the weather is so bad and the water so high that it simply isn't worth fishing. Most of the clients have the sense not to show up when conditions are hopeless, but occasionally one of them will want to go out regardless. Lynn hates fishing when she knows it is a complete waste of time, but if the client wants to go, the client goes and the gillie must go through the motions with a good grace. If February is unsuitable for fishing, Lynn will try to take the odd day off. She needs to get time off when she can, because when the fishing is good, the job is seven days a week. On her rare days off, she will generally help Huw with odd jobs and catch up with the housework, which tends to get neglected. The shooting season finishes on 1 February, so the early part of the month is enlivened by parties for the beaters and pickers up, who have worked on shoot days throughout the season. On days off through the winter, Lynn beats on three different shoots, so she and Huw go to three annual beater's parties. These are the best social gatherings of their year, as the same people tend to beat on the same shoots year after year, so they are rather like a large family.

In March, provided the water level is alright, there is a chance of catching a good fish. The largest fish are caught early in the season, when the water is cold and they tend to sit on the bottom, moving slowly. Only artificial baits like tobies and minnows are used at this time of year and as the fish are lethargic, the fisherman must repeatedly cast his Devon minnow or whatever lure he is using where he thinks the fish may be lying, as a salmon in cold water won't chase a moving bait in the way that it will later in the season. If a lure or minnow is cast over a salmon enough times, it will hopefully entice the salmon to take it.

From mid-April onwards, fishing with natural baits is permitted. This allows those clients who wish to use worms, prawns or shrimps to do so. If the water is still very cold, Lynn and her father will hold off fishing with natural baits until it warms up a little. They collect worms at night, with the aid of a bucket and a torch. On a good night, they can pick up as many as three or four hundred worms in half an hour or so. Fine April weather will bring out canoeists, who can be a major headache for fishermen on the Wye. The majority are well organized and respect fishermen, but some behave incredibly insensitively, crossing the main pools and even swimming in them.

Night-time activities during April are not restricted to collecting worms. The local gillies start organized poacher watches, which are carried out under the auspices of the National Rivers Authority. To augment this channel of liaison and to deal with other problems which specifically affect their local stretch of the Wye, Lynn and her father started a Gillies' Association. During meetings, the gillies on neighbouring beats of the Wye, from Bigsweir to Builth Wells, can discuss problems such as poaching and keep up to date with news of the movements of certain well-known gangs.

When on anti-poaching patrol, Lynn uses surveillance equipment, powerful search lights and two-way radios. Because of the potential threat from poachers who get caught in the act, poacher patrol is always carried out in pairs. The patrols entail sweeping the area, trying to spot anyone behaving suspiciously by the water and sitting in concealed spots, watching for any illicit activity. The gillies have power of search and power of arrest, but first they have to catch up with the poachers, who can be exceedingly sneaky. One evening, Lynn went out on poacher patrol with a stocky lad called Joe, who gillies on another beat. They walked the stretch of the river down from Monmouth Bridge. On the way they spotted a small child sitting on one of the stone cribs – stone walls which project into the river to form pools. They immediately wondered who the child was with and they went down to the water's edge to find out. They saw a man emerge from lower down the bank. He walked right past Lynn, shouting to the child to follow, but her attention was drawn to the water directly below the crib, where she saw a man in a dinghy who appeared to be tying off a net which he had stretched across the river. Joe shouted, 'Stand still, bailiff, come out of the river!' but the man started to row across to the other bank.

Gillies put in long hours trying to catch poachers – sometimes they are out all night, to no avail. Actually to catch a poacher, therefore, is extremely satisfying and Joe was determined not to let this one escape. He thrust his radio and warrant card at Lynn, jumped into the river fully-clothed and started to swim after the dinghy. Lynn, stammering with excitement, got on the radio to her father, who was patrolling further along the bank. He rushed to help. Meanwhile Joe, who had been unable to catch the man he was pursuing, paddled back across the river in the poacher's dinghy. The three of them collected the net and discussed tactics. They figured that the man who had crossed the river couldn't have gone far, so George drove around to the other side, to see if he could spot him. There is an overgrown tributary leading off from this stretch of the river and having a look along this, George spotted the poacher's head, peaking out from some bushes. He lay in wait and in due course, the man walked right past the spot where he was hiding. George grabbed him by the hand and told him he was under arrest. At the police station, the man claimed he had been picking mushrooms. When asked why he was wet, he said untruthfully that it had been raining. The police asked him why he was wet from the shoulders down only. He had no answer. He was charged with poaching. Four nights later, George caught him again. He was prosecuted for both incidents. Sadly, the fines for poaching are not nearly high enough – he was fined only £100.

In May, there is an annual raft race on the Wye. This is a real nuisance for the fisheries. It is a competitive event and one which the competitors take very seriously, practising for weeks beforehand on their rafts, which they construct by lashing oil barrels together. Lynn has had some bad experiences with the rafters, who, far from stopping if she is fishing, have even rammed her. She worries for the baby ducks, who get split off from their mothers as convoy after convoy of rafts come down the river at speed. She hates the litter and mess which they chuck into the river and she finds rafters themselves extremely anti-social. In conservation terms, the race happens at a bad time of year for the river and because of this and the rafters' total lack of consideration towards fishermen, Lynn would cheerfully stick a screwdriver in their barrels.

The disruption to the fishing continues in June when literally hundreds of canoes throng the Wye. Some of the canoeists will ignore signs and requests to stick to one side of the river and will run right over fishing lines, even if the client has a fish on. Lynn itches to smack them with an oar as they pass. As well as accompanying clients, Lynn and her father have to cut weed in June and July, to prevent it choking the river and snaring the boats. They also need to attend to the maintenance of the cribs. They mix concrete and build up worn areas with large stones, topped with sandbags. This is hard work. On one occasion, Lynn and her father shifted thirteen tons of stone from the bank into the river in a single day. Coarse fishing starts in June, although it is discouraged at the Lydbrook Fishery while clients are actually on the river, and mink traps must be laid. As the water level drops in June, so the fishing deteriorates and the number of salmon caught will fall from an average of eight or so a day in May, to maybe four or five. The water is often cloudy with algae.

In July, the fishing is grim. When they are not fishing, the gillies amuse themselves by wearing Polaroid glasses and going out in the boats to see if they can spot salmon in the shallows. They paint the fishing hut, cut the grass and generally concentrate on tidying up. In August, if it rains and the river gets fresh water, the fishing will improve. Natural bait fishing finishes this month and the clients that wish to fish a fly will start now, while others prefer to use Mepps spinners. This are small artificial lures with a rotating blade and treble hook and they can be very effective. The hot summer days are annually enlivened by the Herefordshire Country Fair, where Lynn traditionally enters the fly-casting competitions. She used to win the Ladies' class every year, until she became a professional and was forced to enter the professional class. This is much more demanding as she is competing against the cream of her male counterparts. It is, therefore, greatly to her credit that some years she still manages to win the competition.

In recent years, everyone on the river, including the National Rivers Authority, has been bemoaning the fact that the salmon are becoming smaller. The NRA spent a lot of money on studies exploring the feasibility of producing big salmon artificially in hatcheries and subsequently releasing them into the river. They talked about it a lot, but didn't actually seem to get very far with the project, so Lynn, her father and a few other gillies ambitiously decided to give it a shot themselves. They read up about it and with old tanks and bits and pieces of piping, begged and borrowed from all sorts of sources, they set up their own hatchery in a garage close to the river bank. The tanks and running water system were somewhat Heath Robinson, but they hoped they would prove adequate. Everyone said that they couldn't keep a fish caught on a rod and line alive, but they were determined to give it a try. They acquired the relevant licences to keep and handle fish and they were then ready to make a start. Thereafter, if a client caught a hen fish of 10 lbs or more in August or September, he was asked if it could be taken and used for the hatchery. A small number of the best cock fish were also retained. All of the clients were keen to help and every time they got a suitable fish, Lynn and George transferred it to the tanks in the garage. To their delight, although they lost some, the majority of them survived.

In December, when a hen fish was 'ripe' with eggs, George and Lynn lifted her carefully out of the tank. They tied a noose around her neck to stop her wriggling and stroked her belly to strip the eggs out of her. She was then released back into the river. The cock fish were similarly stripped and the eggs were fertilized in hatchery trays. On a daily basis, Lynn would check the eggs and remove any bad ones. After a while she could see eyes starting to develop in the eggs and after ninety days, to her excitement, she found little pink things swimming around in the running water. They had produced their first baby salmon. After a couple of weeks these 'alvins', as they are called, began to look like proper little fish. With great pride, they put some back into the river, but because of the threat from things that would eat them, such as pike, trout, kingfishers and mergansers, they kept a lot back and reared them for a year until they reached a safer size for release. These grew into perfectly formed miniature salmon. It was a delight to watch them swimming around in the home-made rearing tanks. Even at a year old, there was a marked size difference among the individuals. With the help of the NRA, who were most impressed by this pioneering effort, the young fish were micro-tagged before being released. With the aid of the micro-tags, they can be traced to see if they return the following year and to see what size they are. In undertaking this exercise, Lynn feels that she and her father have really achieved something worthwhile – they have made a contribution to the sport they love and in doing so they have also done something which others said was impossible.

In September the fishing begins to improve. If the hen fish are not being kept for the hatchery, they are put back into the river. On

17 October the season closes. The following weekend the boats are taken out of the water and all the equipment is stowed in the garage at the back of the fishery. Although she loves fishing, the end of the season has always come as something of a relief to Lynn – gillieing hours are long and hard and the close season provides a welcome opportunity to concentrate on maintenance, uninterrupted by long hours on the water. The boats are painted in November and December, in readiness for the next season. The winter months are enlivened by coarse fishing, the odd day's beating on local shoots and maybe a holiday in Scotland, during which Lynn and Huw can go stalking. On one occasion, they even went on a memorable safari in Kenya. As the nights draw in, Lynn will head for the fireside in the evenings to tie flies and reload bullets for her rifle – an exacting and potentially dangerous pastime, but nevertheless one which she relishes.

After Christmas, which Lynn really enjoys, January is the month of serious preparation for the opening of the season once more. The gillies will visit their local tackle shop to stock up, they will get the boats back on to the water and they must show the fishery to any potential clients. If the water looks promising, there is an air of anticipation on the river, as everyone fantasizes about the unlikely chance of catching a seriously large fish on the opening day of the season.

Suddenly, for Lynn, there was no opening day of the 1993 season. Mrs Plaice had died in the summer of 1991. Mr Plaice abruptly lost interest in the fishery and on 3 December 1992 – ironically also Lynn's birthday – the fishery was sold at auction to Mr and Mrs Wilson, a couple who loved their fishing and had plans to fish it every weekend of the season. The Wilsons went to see Lynn and George and, to the latter's horror, they explained that they had no interest in letting the fishing and consequently that they wouldn't need any gillies. Deeply shocked, Lynn and her father considered their options. The first priority was George. Lynn was young enough to find other work, but the river was George's life. After much consideration, he went back to see the Wilsons. The upshot was that they made a deal.

George would gillie for them when they fished at weekends and he would continue to maintain the river, in return for being allowed to let nine rods on weekdays, when the Wilsons wouldn't be fishing anyway, and retain the income to provide himself with a living.

This arrangement was a godsend for her father, but sadly, it didn't help Lynn as the income yielded from the lets was not sufficient to support both of them. Initially, Lynn couldn't believe that they didn't want her. She was a first-class gillie and she had devoted herself to the river for the last five years. What on earth could she do? Unfortunately, the best she could do was to get a job as a night porter in a hotel in nearby Ross-on-Wye. In a manner reminiscent of her schooldays, she is now reduced to heading down to the river at lunchtime, or in the evenings before going to work, to see how the fishermen have got on. She misses the job terribly and the clients miss her. Some still ask for her to take them out any day that she can make it and this she does with alacrity whenever she can.

Fishing is and always will be her passion. Despite her new job, during the 1993 season she managed to fish a total of ten days and to catch an impressive score of eight fish. In the future, she and Huw would like to get married, have children and possibly to move to Scotland, which has everything they love, but Lynn is an only child and she is aware of the gap it would leave in her parents' life if she moved that far away. Her immediate problem, however, is her career. She aches for the freedom of being able to work outside once more. Above all, she is a countrywoman and before she is stifled in a workplace which is totally unsuitable for her, she desperately needs to find another job in the country. As jobs go, she is acutely aware of the one which got away. 'I was very happy doing the job – who can get paid to do a job like that? People pay hundreds and thousands of pounds to fish one day a week and there was me fishing seven days a week and getting paid for it!' She thinks she is unlikely to find another Mr Plaice, prepared to take a chance on a female gillie, but in a perfect world, she would like to head for another river, where the fishing is really good . . .

'Naturally, I'd like to go somewhere where we would catch an awful lot of fish because I just love fishing. I really can't imagine anything else but wanting to be a gillie.'

CHAPTER 6

Emma Ford

FALCONER

High above me, my falcon hangs on the wind, intently watching every movement in the heather below. As I move a few paces, she drifts forward to stay directly over me, almost as if she was attached to me by a gossamer thread. The dog, patiently holding his point, stiffens, then creeps forward a little too – the grouse must be running through the heather. There is a momentary pause, then a burst of activity as I call to the dog, 'Get 'em up!' The dog rushes forward and the grouse burst from the heather. The falcon turns against the wind and plummets downwards in her stoop. As the wind screams through her feathers, she closes in behind a grouse and gathers it sweetly into her talons. She turns into the wind to break her momentum and descends into the heather.

I was born on 27 February 1962 in Canterbury, Kent. My father, Arthur Braham, was the senior partner in a firm of solicitors and my parents lived in Japonica Cottage, in the rural hamlet of Lynsted in Kent. At the time my father was building a house in the same village and when I was a few months old it was completed, and my parents and I and my brother Charlie – who is five years older than me –

145

moved into Medlar House, just across the fields. It was a beautiful house with six bedrooms, set in an acre and a half of gardens.

My earliest memory is of being in my pram at the bottom of the garden and of Major, the family's Alsatian, with his paws up on the pram's handle, peering in at me. Unfortunately, Major developed a penchant for pulling passing cyclists off their bicycles and he had to be passed on to a new home, where he would be kept in a kennel. After Major, my parents got a St Bernard called Heidi. Heidi was a gentle, good-humoured dog and the family was soon besotted with her. In the garden there were two large symmetrical banks, formed from the soil which had been taken out from the footings of the house. In the snow, Charlie and I would toboggan down the face of one bank and attempt to get up the face of the next. Heidi, always in her element in the snow, would sit in the gap between the banks and try to knock us off our toboggans as we passed. This she could do merely by lifting one huge paw and banging on the front rail of the toboggan. If she managed to dislodge one of us into the snow, she would stroll over and lie on the luckless individual, who was thus rendered completely helpless.

Heidi grew so big that she made moving around the kitchen, where she lived, extremely hazardous. Slow-moving and amiable, if ejected from the kitchen to the garden, she would find one of the gardeners and lean against him, effectively preventing him from doing any work. As she was totally untrained, she was unresponsive to all commands and cries of 'Sit!' 'Stay!' or 'Lie down!' were greeted with a blank stare. Charlie and I spent many hours trying to train her to fetch a ball, but she moved at only two speeds – dead slow and stop – and she wasn't interested in physical exertion of any kind. She would watch the ball disappear into the distance and we would have to go and pick it up ourselves.

As she became more and more of a hindrance, both in the house and in the garden, my parents decided they had to relocate her. They didn't want to kennel her, so finally my father decided to build an extension on the house. The result was a vast and impressive building, which in later life became a second dining room, known as the 'Heidi

House'. Sadly, shortly after it was completed, Heidi became sick with pyometra – an infection of the womb – and despite several operations and some devoted nursing from my mother, she had to be put to sleep, to the devastation of the family.

To fill the yawning gap in our lives, my father got not one but two St Bernard puppies, which were named Porgy and Bess. Aged seven, I used to attempt to take them for walks on the lead, but they would both pull in different directions and I would feel as though I was being yanked in half. I adored animals and birds of all kinds, so my mother let me keep pigeons – an ornate and colourful variety called bald-headed tumblers. In addition, I used to rescue sick or injured wildlife. Anything I found I would keep in a box under my bed, where I could give the creature constant love and attention. This was not a habit my father approved of, especially as these waifs and strays frequently used to die and I would be distraught. One day I left the door to my bedroom open. I was keeping a sick feral pigeon in the box and the family cat got in and ate the bird. The mess was indescribable – the pigeon had clearly made a bid for freedom when the cat pushed the lid off the box and there was evidence of a good chase before the pigeon finally succumbed, in a sticky mess of blood and feathers. Thereafter, I was banned from keeping animals in my bedroom.

My first school was a convent in nearby Sittingbourne. I worked extremely hard and generally got good results. This was in complete contrast to Charlie, who was very bright but absolutely bone idle. He boarded at his prep school and I only saw him on the occasional weekend and during school holidays. The latter invariably got off to a bad start when Charlie arrived home clasping his end-of-term report. The comments therein would reduce my father to a state of apoplexy. My favourite of all time read: 'Braham's snail-like progress towards half term has since ceased.'

When I was eight years old, my world fell apart. My father had gone away for a few days and I overheard my mother talking on the telephone in the next room – 'somewhere small with a nice garden would do . . .' she was saying. I walked into the room and she looked at me and put the phone down, looking very sad. 'Darling, I'm so sorry you heard that – I'm divorcing your father,' she told me, without further preamble. 'He will stay in this house and we will move to somewhere smaller.' To add to my misery, the puppies, Porgy and Bess, couldn't stay at Medlar House with no one there in the day time and I was told that they would be too big to come with us, so they were sent back to the breeder. In the middle of winter, we moved out of the luxury of Medlar House into an unheated but charming cottage called Carpenters, on the edge of the Chilham Castle Estate, about twenty miles away.

There were no other children living within walking distance and Charlie was still away at school, so I had a rather isolated existence. I moved schools to Ashford School for Girls, which I loathed, although I continued to work hard. My mother had very little money and we lived frugally, although she did her best to see that I had a really good childhood – I was forever bringing home friends from school to stay the night. However, I remember really grasping how hard up we were when my mother said to me, 'I'm afraid that you are going to have to stop bringing people home from school – you see when they eat, I don't.' I felt incredibly guilty and it awakened me early to the realities of money and making ends meet.

Three months after we had moved, new neighbours arrived at the house next door. Curious to catch sight of them, I popped my head over their garden wall and came eyeball-to-eyeball with a falcon. It was sitting on a perch on the lawn and I was completely captivated by it. It had large, dark liquid eyes and long pointed wings, held open to the breeze. I thought it was the most beautiful thing I had ever seen and I wanted to get closer to it. The falconer, Alan Oswald, saw me and came over to talk. He explained that the hawk I was admiring was a lanner falcon. He added that he had a number of birds of prey and that he was going to introduce falconry demonstrations to the grounds of Chilham Castle, as an attraction for visitors.

Alan and his wife Ann were very good to me. I was much keener on the hawks than either of their two sons were and, perhaps as a result of this, they were willing to teach me. I spent hours next door, mesmerized by the hawks, which ranged in size from two kestrels up to a magnificent imperial eagle called Bugsy. I learned how to handle the hawks, how to gut rabbits and prepare food for them and when Wally, a Walhberg's eagle arrived to join the collection, Alan generously said that I could train him. Despite his size, I had no fear of Wally. Like most children, I lacked the sense of self-preservation which is instinctively possessed by most adults. I would get up very early before school to collect Wally from the mews – the hawk house – next door. In the peaceful hours before the general public were admitted to the grounds of the castle, I would walk with him on my gloved fist around the lake to tame or 'man' him.

When my mother felt I was ready to take on the responsibility of my own hawk, I had a succession of birds which I kept in my tiny home-made mews, constructed out of a wooden Wendy house which had been left in our garden by the previous owners. My first hawk was Jasper, a crane hawk acquired from a zoological suppliers. Crane hawks came from South America, where they specialize in catching snakes in crevices with their long, double-jointed legs. This was hardly a suitable hunting partner for a small girl in the Kent countryside, but I trained him anyway and had just got him flying when he died of coccidiosis – a worm infestation which, had I been more knowledgeable, I could easily have treated.

I missed Jasper terribly and blamed myself, reading anything I could lay my hands on to improve my knowledge of hawk husbandry, but the only books on falconry available then were dated, or in some cases ancient manuscripts which listed old-fashioned cures for maladies in hawks, which were described under quaint headings such as 'snurt' and 'croaks and kecks'. In due course, I had other hawks, including a common buzzard with which I used to attempt to hunt rabbits on the castle estate, but it took me a long time to get over the death of Jasper.

We were still very short of money so, aged nine, I took a job after school, at weekends and throughout the school holidays to support my hawks. I worked for Ann Oswald in the gift shop and tea rooms at the castle for fifty pence a week. I sat behind the till, made sandwiches, served endless cups of tea, washed up and sold countless ice creams and trinkets to tourists. My mother took in a lodger to help make ends meet. It was through the lodger that I managed to get a small role in a feature film, at the age of ten. The lodger knew the casting director for a Lyndsay Anderson film called *Oh Lucky Man* and the casting director selected me to spend three days working on location at a nearby church, playing the role of the vicar's daughter. The star of the film was Malcolm McDowell and I had a small speaking part with him. My mother accompanied me as chaperone and we had a wonderful three days, enjoying the lavish film catering almost as much as we enjoyed the experience of watching a large international film crew at work. To top it all, we got paid £30 per day, which seemed like a small fortune.

My parent's divorce had turned acrimonious over the question of custody and 'care and control' of Charlie and me. Finally, I had to go to court to explain that I was happy with my mother. For the next seven years I hardly saw my father, who had remarried. In 1975 an elderly relative of my father died and left a small legacy to my mother. This financial windfall made all the difference to us and although my mother still had to be careful with money, we managed much better. We took the odd holiday and when I was twelve years old one of these, to my delight, took us down to the Falconry Centre in Newent, Gloucestershire. At the time, this centre was owned by Phillip Glasier – a well-known falconer who had a wonderful collection of birds of prey for flying and breeding. To me, it was Mecca. Recognizing my enthusiasm, with great kindness Phillip taught me to train longwings – members of the falcon family. There are many different branches of the sport of falconry, each one relating to the type of hawk being flown. Longwings are swift-flying aerial hunters which prey on other birds and include amongst their number our native peregrine. As I mastered the basics of training falcons under Phillip's watchful eye and read avidly about my craft every evening, I knew that one day I wanted to fly my own peregrines against the toughest of all our native quarry species, the red grouse.

One day, when I was fourteen years old, a noise from the

paddock at the back of the cottage caught my attention. I looked out of the window to see a number of horses careering around the field, ridden energetically and with great flamboyance by young men dressed in jeans and cowboy hats. I loved riding – I had learned to ride when I first moved to Chilham, on Pharaoh – a seventeen-hand, heavy-weight hunter which belonged to an elderly man in the village. Pharaoh had died a couple of years later and since then I had had few opportunities to ride, so the sudden sight of a number of beautiful horses right outside the house immediately captured my interest. But I was intrigued even more by one of the young men riding. He rode with great expertise and, as far as I could see, he was extremely good-looking, with long blonde hair emerging from under a black Stetson. I watched him for about half an hour as he exercised his horse, then, to my disappointment, he disappeared back into the old brick stable yard, which belonged to the castle and which had not been in use since my mother and I had arrived in the cottage.

At the time, I used to take the Oswalds' hawks to the medieval banquets which were held in the Norman Keep at Chilham Castle every Friday and Saturday night. The following Friday, I went up to the banquet with Wally, as usual, to earn the few pounds which I received for handing Wally over to guests so that they could have their photographs taken with him. All week I had not been able to get the mysterious young rider out of my mind and I was therefore surprised and delighted to be introduced to him when I arrived. His name, I learned, was Steve. He was nineteen years old and he was shortly going to move into a room in the stable yard, as groom for the Jousting Association of Great Britain, which was scheduled to add to the tourist attractions at the castle that year. I was amazed to learn that prior to joining the Jousting Association, Steve had been the head falconer at the Hawking Centre in Crediton, Devon.

We hit it off right from the start. I invited him down to supper and from that evening onwards, we never looked back. My mother liked Steve immediately and pretty soon he was eating with us every evening. It was 1977 and he was earning only twenty pounds a week, plus his room, which had a piece of polythene rick sheet on the floor as a carpet, a string across one corner for his clothes and a massive stone sink. A little room off this housed a concrete-floored shower and a loo. He had no fridge and every Saturday, I would wash up a week's worth of dirty crocks, piled high in the sink, invariably finding a couple of green milk bottles at the bottom.

I fell deeply in love with Steve and when I was fifteen, I asked my mother to let him move in with us. I told her that I knew for certain that he was the one for me, that one day we would get married and that if she let him stay she would never have to go through the worry of me going out on dates in the evening, or have to put up with any of the typical teenage daughter traumas, as she would always know exactly where I was and who I was with. After due consideration, she agreed. Whilst my contemporaries at school were endlessly talking about who was going out with whom and which discos they were going to at the weekend, I enjoyed the distinction of being the only fifteen-year-old who was picked up from school by my boyfriend, driving my mother's car.

Around this time, the Oswalds left Chilham, taking their collection of hawks with them. I missed the birds terribly and Steve and I decided to build up our own collection of hawks in the back garden at Carpenters. I contacted Phillip Glasier at the Falconry Centre and asked if he had any hawks which he would be prepared to sell to us. He replied that he had a long-legged buzzard 'twiddling her bloody toes' on a perch and that if we wanted her, we could give him a donation of fifty pounds towards his aviary fund. Steve could earn ten pounds extra on his wages by doing a choreographed 'saddle fall' during the jousting displays at the weekends. He had recently been doing as many as possible in order to save up to buy hawks. Combined with my savings from the banquets, we had just enough, so I took a day off school and Steve, my mother and I travelled down to Gloucestershire to pick up our new acquisition, whom we had decided to call 'Ebony'.

Ebony is one of the best things which has ever happened to us. We trained her and she was soon catching rabbits, doing demonstrations, banquets and filmwork. She was the foundation of our business and we called ourselves 'The Bird of Prey Centre'. As the collection expanded, we started to give demonstrations at local events. We attracted attention from the media and were featured in magazine and newspaper articles and gave television and radio interviews. The business began to snowball. One of the highlights of these early years was a booking to supply hawks, including the stalwart Ebony, for the feature film *Dracula*, directed by John Badham, of *Saturday Night Fever* fame. We agreed a fee of £250 for the day's filming, plus all expenses. We travelled first-class on British Rail down to Cornwall. As the train stopped at Exeter station, Steve's parents, whom we rarely had the opportunity to see, saw us briefly and thrust home-made Cornish pasties through the window. We then travelled on to Penzance where we were shown up to a palatial hotel suite for us and the hawks. The filming was taking place on St Michael's Mount – an island off the coast of Penzance, joined to the mainland by a causeway which was only passable at low tide. We were driven out across the causeway in the morning and we filmed until lunchtime, when we were amazed to discover that the caterers had managed to get two enormous catering wagons out across the causeway and were serving a location lunch of roast lamb with all the trimmings. After lunch, we filmed until late into the evening and the hawks behaved immaculately, but whilst we were filming the tide came in and when we finished, we had to be taken back with the hawks to the mainland in a small boat. We returned home the following day and eagerly awaited the arrival of the cheque. When it came, it was for £750 – we had been paid in full for the travelling days too! We worked several more days on the same production at Shepperton Studios and the money we earned enabled us to build up our collection of hawks far more quickly than we had envisaged.

When I was fifteen, Steve arranged with my mother to take me back to Medlar House to see my father. We had been out of touch for so long that I really didn't know what to expect. What I found was a tall, handsome man with a first-class and highly respected legal mind. He explained that although he had missed me terribly, he had realized that it was essential for my mother to keep Charlie and me to herself for a few years and he had waited patiently, knowing that one day he would see me again on a regular basis. Shortly after I was reunited with my father, he was diagnosed as having cancer. It suddenly became painfully clear to me just how much time I had lost with him and that now I would only know my father with the shadow of cancer hanging over him.

My life at this time was a medieval existence of hawks, horses, tournaments and banquets. I spent as much time as possible training hawks and in the evenings, if we didn't have a booking for a banquet, which we had taken over when the Oswalds left, we would take Ebony hunting across the castle estate. Anything she caught helped to feed her, the other hawks and if there was enough, us too. I was still at school, but had been attending less and less as the business grew. Sometimes, I would go into school just for the morning, then, without saying a word to anyone, quietly catch a train home at lunchtime. I was never caught or questioned and I needed to get home to deal with the growing mountain of business paperwork. Meanwhile, Steve and my mother helped me out with my homework. Steve used to do all my biology diagrams and was delighted when he got better marks for them than he used to when he was at school.

Having completed eight 'O' levels, I didn't want to stay at school to do two years of 'A' levels. I really didn't want to take 'A' levels at all and while all my friends were working out which university they wanted to go to, all I wanted to do was to join Steve in the business. I had learned early in life that it was important to earn one's keep and I could see no point in wasting time on further education. However, my parents, despite their differences, were in total accord that I should follow a professional career. For years, my mother had wanted me to read medicine. I didn't want to go away to medical school for the next seven years, so finally we compromised and agreed that I should study law – not at university but by postal degree course, which I could complete whilst simultaneously being articled to a local firm. I left school and went to Canterbury Technical College to get my 'A' levels in one year instead of two.

I was on the bus one Monday morning heading for college, when a woman waiting at a bus stop en route fainted on to the pavement. Everyone on the bus looked out of the window and commented, but to my utter amazement, neither the bus driver nor any of the other passengers made a move to help her. I leapt off the bus to go to her aid. I scooped her up as best I could and she recovered sufficiently to tell me that she lived in a nearby farm cottage. I supported her as we walked the short distance to her home and to my relief, her husband was there, so I was able to pass her over to his care. The bus had left immediately I got off, so I started to walk back to Chilham, which was about five miles away. It was obviously destined to be a strange morning, because as I was walking, I came across a black and white puppy, which looked like a border collie cross, trying to eat grit at the side of the main road. He saw me coming and started to crawl on his belly towards me, wagging his tail in an ingratiating manner. He was not wearing a collar. As he was clearly lost and dicing with death by being on the edge of the road, I looped my belt around his neck and took him home. Steve was surprised to see me back so soon and even more surprised to see my canine companion. I phoned the police and they told me that a car had been seen over the weekend out of which had been thrown a black and white kitten and a black and white puppy. It had then driven off. The desk sergeant said that if I wanted to take the dog down to the station, it would be kept for a week, then if it wasn't claimed, it would be put down. Steve and I decided that if the dog wasn't claimed we'd keep him. We called him Havoc and he proved to be a great character and a devoted companion for the next six years.

When our collection of hawks was large enough, Steve was able to take over the position of falconer at the castle and stop throwing himself off horses for a living. The position came with a house – North Lodge – one of Chilham Castle's two gatehouses, which overlooked the beautiful square of Chilham village. We moved out of Carpenters and into our first home when I was sixteen. While I was still at college, Steve did six flying displays a day at the castle. He also ran falconry courses – something which we had started to do whilst still at

Carpenters. We felt strongly that the route into falconry for a beginner should not be to acquire a hawk, buy a book and see if the rest could be figured out. In addition, the sport had given us a great deal of pleasure and we wanted to give other people the chance to share in it. Phillip Glasier had been the first person to run falconry courses at his centre, but these were only run during the winter months. We decided to offer courses all the year round, on a residential basis. Students stayed with us in North Lodge and I cooked and cleaned for them when I returned from college.

When I was still only sixteen, I was given the opportunity to write a book on falconry. A photographer – Robert Hallmann – who had been coming to Chilham to photograph the hawks for the last couple of years, submitted his portfolio of photographs to a publisher and suggested that they could be used in a book. The publisher liked the idea but asked Robert for a suggestion as to who should write it. He asked me if I would like to and I jumped at the chance. I sent a sample chapter in to the publisher and they gave me a six-month contract to write a seventy-thousand word technical manual. I decided to call the book, *Falconry in Mews and Field* and I set to work. A short time later the same publishers, Batsford, asked me to write a second book – a ten-thousand word paperback called *Birds of Prey*, to join a full-colour series which they were producing at the time. The only snag was that to tie in with the other books in the series which were being produced at the same time as a job lot in Italy, I would have to complete this one in ten days. I accepted this condition and managed to get the manuscript in on schedule by the skin of my teeth.

While I was writing the books, I was still at college, but I was increasingly aware of the fact that I didn't want to spend the rest of my life as a lawyer. I had tremendous faith in the work which Steve and I were doing and I was certain that we could make a living at it for both of us. I tackled my parents. I was fortunate that I had been asked to write the books as this seemed somehow to make our endeavours respectable and to my delight, they agreed, with the proviso that I should complete my two 'A' levels. This I duly did, passing English and History.

In late 1979 Steve and I were featured in an article in the *Daily Telegraph*. The article was seen by the Bank of Credit and Commerce International in London, who at the time had HRH Sheikh Zaid bin Sultan al Nahayan the ruler of Abu Dhabi and the President of the United Arab Emirates as one of their customers. The bank decided that it might interest Sheikh Zaid to meet a young couple from England who shared his passion for falconry – apparently the younger men in his own country were no longer interested in the ancient Arabic tradition of falconry, now that they had fast cars and all the other trappings of wealth in the oil-rich Gulf States. The upshot of it was that the bank offered Steve and me an expenses-paid trip to Abu Dhabi to meet Sheikh Zaid and to talk to him about falconry and about breeding falcons in captivity – to date we had managed to produce a number of young falcons from our own pairs, whereas he had not attempted to breed his own falcons. It proved to be the trip of a lifetime. I was seventeen and Steve was twenty-two.

We flew out first-class with British Airways and we were put into the Abu Dhabi Hilton, with carte blanche. We met Sheikh Zaid three times during our week in the Gulf and I had to become an honorary man in order to be allowed into his palaces. I was referred to as 'Mr Braham'. Our trip took place in November when his falcons were in training, in preparation for the forthcoming hunting season. He had 150 falcons that year, in the care of 150 falconers. We talked through an interpreter and in the evenings we would go out into the desert to watch the falcons being called. At sunset, we sat in the middle of a huge circle of falconers, interspersed with bodyguards holding rifles – it was just after Iran had fallen and security in the Middle East at the time was very tight. Sheikh Zaid's falconers were clearly puzzled by me – in their country no women flew falcons. Although I tried to have contact with their birds, initially they shielded them from me. Then one elderly man held out his saker falcon for me to stroke. She sunk her beak into my finger and they all laughed. I left my finger there and she soon stopped biting. Immediately, their attitude towards me changed – they were much more friendly after that.

The highlight of the trip came when Sheikh Zaid, studying a photograph of one of our baby falcons, offered us a job. He told us that we could design a breeding station close to one of his palaces in the desert and that we would have a house, staff, cars and a helicopter, as well as a salary of £48,000 a year. We were told to go home to England, get married – as we could not live together in Abu Dhabi unless we were husband and wife – and prepare to return the following spring. Stunned, we shopped in the souks to buy our wedding rings and returned to England, complete with two gold Rolex watches which he had given to us as a gift.

We had planned to get married late in 1980, but we brought the wedding forward to February, just before my eighteenth birthday. Just before we got married, ITV screened a programme entitled *The Death of a Princess*, which told the story of the execution of a Middle Eastern princess. Diplomatic relations between Britain and the Middle East took a nosedive overnight and many British business contracts were lost, including ours.

It took us a long time to get over this setback. We had been earning a very small salary at Chilham – £2,600 a year to support us and all the hawks, plus anything extra which we could make through the banquets and courses. Out of the blue, this opportunity to work in the Gulf had cropped up, only to be snatched away from us through no fault of our own. We sat back and took a long, hard look at our life and we realized that we didn't want to spend the rest of our days living in someone else's house giving falconry demonstrations. What we really wanted to do was to open a school of falconry where we could specialize in teaching the sport we loved. My mother, who had recently remarried, came to the rescue. She bought us a cottage set on a couple of acres of level ground in the nearby village of Stelling Minnis. We sold our Rolex watches and bought our first peregrine with the proceeds and with three courses booked, seventy pounds in our pockets and a good dose of faith in our vision of the future, we moved and opened the British School of Falconry in 1982.

Steve and I worked hard on designing and building a complex for our hawks which we could be really proud of. With blood, sweat, tears and a lot of fence panels, chainlink mesh and staples, we built an enclosed, rectangular weathering ground, with nineteen individual, three-sided, roofed shelters for our trained hawks and twelve breeding aviaries for our pairs. We completed this structure in thirty days by working late into the night with the aid of torchlight. We decorated the cottage, prepared bedrooms for the students and on the day we opened for one bemused little boy, the local television station was there to cover the event. The media snowball began to roll and we had so much publicity that in the first year we taught one hundred and fifteen students on week-long residential courses.

My books were published in the same year. I came in for a lot of flack from other falconers – all male and all members of the British Falconer's Club, who believed that the sport should not be brought to the attention of a wider public, but remain as 'a minority sport for a small group of gentlemen'. My detractors were all much older than me and clearly outraged that this young girl should encroach on their territory. Whilst I had super letters and phone calls from inexperienced falconers all over the country, saying how much the books had helped them, my reviews, written by the aforementioned 'old school' falconers made comments such as, 'young folks may clasp this book to their bosom, but older folks will be less enthusiastic.' Years later, when we were filming for the BBC, I met the falconer who had written this review, Dick Treleaven. He admired the peregrines I was flying for the filming, apologized for the review and admitted that he had been encouraged by senior members of the British Falconer's Club to do a 'hatchet' job on the book. As a rider to this story, I am happy to report that I am now a member of the club and my relationship with its senior members has greatly improved!

As the courses went from strength to strength, we regularly filled our quota of four residential students per week and we were able to take on staff, including a housekeeper and a secretary, which spared me from juggling teaching with the escalating load of paperwork and domestic duties, which up until that point had included cooking for students. I took a contract to work for Maher Al Tajir, the eldest son of the former Ambassador to the United Arab Emirates. Maher's family owned a castle one hour's drive away from the school and I was engaged to breed and fly falcons for him. I worked for him seven days a week from 1984 to 1989 and I learned a great deal, not only from the work I was doing with the falcons, but also about money and business. It was through this contract that Steve and I started to go up to Scotland each year to fly peregrines at grouse. I would spend three or four months a year in Perthshire, staying in a massive house owned by Maher's family and Steve would join me when he could. Not only did we thereby achieve our lifetime ambition to go grouse hawking each season, but we also fell deeply in love with Scotland. One day, we decided, we would live there.

Periodically, Charlie would come to stay with us. Although as a small boy he had always loved the country and had also learned how to fly hawks, he had not been as fortunate as I had in terms of being able to carve out a life for himself in a rural environment. His scholastic career had ended abruptly, when he had been expelled from Tonbridge School for spending too much time in the tuck shop instead of attending lessons. He had had a number of temporary jobs in the intervening years, but had found nothing which could hold his attention. Finally he had managed to find a niche in something which he had enjoyed from childhood – namely toys. He was now working in a model shop and, having found a job which he really liked, he was applying himself to it with uncharacteristic dedication. I always enjoyed Charlie's visits because although he and I are very different in terms of our ambitions, we have always got on extremely well and share the same sense of humour.

Living cheek by jowl with students and staff week in, week out, was far from ideal and one of the major drawbacks in our life at that time was that Steve and I had little privacy. We decided to rectify this by getting planning permission to build another house on our land. We designed a large Scandinavian timber-framed house and in 1988, this was completed. We moved in, leaving the courses running in the cottage as before. Shortly afterwards, I gave up the contract with Maher so that Steve and I could spend more time together, concentrating on our rapidly-expanding business. Mackenzie House, as we called our new home, was sheer luxury and reminded me a lot of Medlar House which I had left as a child.

I employed a top-rate personal assistant called Penny, who worked with me for the next seven years. These were exciting times, as when the phone rang, we never knew whether it would be a booking for a course, a film job, the offer of another book to write, a journalist or a contract to work overseas. We enjoyed many accolades – I was invited annually to attend the Women of the Year Luncheon at the Savoy and in 1989, I was voted Countrywoman of the Year by the *Daily Express*. At long last, too, Steve and I were able to take time off together to go grouse hawking for our own pleasure. From 1989, for three years, we rented a beautiful cottage in Doune in Perthshire and nearby Braco Castle moor for our hawking. Every August we packed the Range Rover to the roof and headed north, complete with hawks, pointers, fishing rods and shotguns for three glorious months of sport.

One year, Sheikh Rashid bin Khalifa al Maktoum, a member of the ruling family of Dubai, decided that he wanted to come with us to Scotland for a few weeks. He is an expert falconer in his own right, but he wanted to see how we trained captive-bred falcons, as opposed to the wild-trapped birds which are favoured by the Arabs. He had two companions with him and together they were going to stay in a house on the same estate as our cottage.

After we arrived, Amtrak delivered three huge boxes of cooking equipment and an impressive range of herbs and spices which Rashid had had sent up to cook with for the duration of 'falcon camp', as he called it. We spent many happy evenings exercising falcons in preparation for the 'Glorious Twelfth' of August when the grouse hawking opens. Rashid was fascinated to see how rapidly the young captive-bred peregrines improved as they built up muscle, and each evening he would settle happily in the training field, surrounded by the pointers, to watch the falcons' progress.

When we fly our peregrines, we fit them with a small transmitter which we attach to their tails. This device enables us to track them if they are lost. The transmitter is fixed to a special mount on the tail with an electrical cable tie, which is clipped off with a pair of toenail clippers after use. I was mildly amused to see Rashid remove his sandals one evening while watching the falcons and start clipping his toenails. But amusement turned to embarrassment when Duke, one of the pointers, wandered over and started to eat the clippings, making loud crunching noises as he devoured the bits of toenail, which kept getting stuck in his teeth.

Altogether, it was an unorthodox start to the season, filled with laughter and enlivened by some excellent Arabic cooking. When the Glorious Twelfth dawned, we phoned Rashid to say that we wanted to head for the moor at about eleven-thirty that morning, as soon as the falcons had finished bathing and preening. Eleven-thirty came and went and by twelve o'clock there was still no sign of him. He finally showed up apologetically at twenty past twelve muttering something about lunch. We headed for the moor and after the first couple of flights, we returned to the vehicles to change falcons. Rashid enquired if we were now stopping for lunch. Thinking he meant a quick sandwich, we said yes, fine. To our astonishment, his companions produced a massive, steaming tub of rice and meat from the back of his Range Rover, where it had been wrapped in towels to keep it warm. We sat cross-legged in the heather, eating this substantial repast with our hands. After we had finished, his companions produced a bottle of mineral water, soap and a towel for us to wash our hands. Replete, we resumed our hawking, reflecting that traditional habits from the desert seemed somewhat bizarre on the grouse moors of Scotland.

In 1988, our travels took us further afield. We were asked by the Jurong Birdpark in Singapore – reputed to be the best bird park in the world – to spend three months there, setting up bird-of-prey flying demonstrations for their visitors. We flew out to Singapore and discovered to our delight that the Birdpark was a beautiful environment in which to work. The lush, tropical vegetation provided the perfect backdrop for the vivid and varied colours of this sensational collection of birds. Whilst we acclimatized ourselves to working in Singapore's steamy heat, we were given an area of the park to develop into a hawk walk, a flying arena and a museum, as well as twelve staff to train. We were also given access to the park's aviary stock of birds of prey, ranging from owls to vultures. Some of these birds had been in aviaries for twenty years or more and it was our task to select individuals for training. We chose a white-bellied sea eagle, two king vultures, a wedge-tailed eagle and some Harris hawks. These we combined with a lanner falcon, which we had imported from England, to set up a unique natural behaviour show, which we entitled 'The Kings of the Skies'.

If the multi-racial residents of Singapore glance upwards past their skyscrapers from time to time, they may well see a large bird of prey pass overhead, as there are many wild hawks breeding on the island. The vast majority of Singaporeans, however, have no idea about the natural habits of raptors and it was this aspect that the Birdpark specifically wanted us to address, in an educational but entertaining format. We therefore attempted not merely to show the trained birds in flight, but to simulate how they hunted or scavenged. We dug a small pond in the flying arena and trained the white-bellied sea eagle to snatch fish from the surface of the water. We had a fibreglass carcass of a dead deer made up and taught the king vultures to fly into the arena, land, run over and feed from this model by putting their heads right inside to find pieces of meat. We used traditional falconry techniques to show the lanner falcon 'stooping to the lure' – chasing a pair of bird wings swung by the falconer – and a Harris hawk chasing and catching a dummy rabbit. We opened the show just before we left the Birdpark, to an invited audience of one thousand, including government ministers, ambassadors and other VIPs. The Singaporeans we had taught continued to do the shows for visitors to the Birdpark on a daily basis after we left.

The show was so popular that we were asked back three more times to put together other shows for the Birdpark. We introduced new 'acts', including an Andean condor – the world's largest flying bird with a wingspan of over ten feet and an ancient Egyptian vulture whom we found lurking in an aviary. Egyptian vultures are one of nature's tool-users: they eat eggs by breaking them open with a stone, held firmly in their beaks. We couldn't persuade Rod Stewart – our

Egyptian vulture – to use a stone, but he would grasp a chicken's egg in his beak and drop it on a concrete slab to break it. He would then slurp up the contents with evident enjoyment.

During our final trip to Singapore in 1990 we put together a much more ambitious package for the Birdpark. In their air-conditioned auditorium we devised a show which included a combination of video, audio-visual techniques and live action. The whole programme was set to music and a natural history commentary, and was run by computer. We devised the show, wrote the script, acquired sponsorship for it from Sony and Fuji and, together with a professional production company, shot footage for it and edited it. It was the first production in the world to combine these elements.

Back at home, our work with teaching and with our hawks continued. Since 1979 we had owned a golden eagle, called Sebastian. He was one of the nicest mannered, most tolerant eagles I have ever had the good fortune to encounter. Small children could pat him on the head and he would behave as beautifully indoors on the gloved fist or on a perch as he would outside, hunting. He also flew like a dream. In the highlands of Scotland, he would fly like a wild eagle, circling high above the mountain peaks, but all the time under perfect control, stooping back to the glove or lure the moment he was called. With this amazing bird, we were able to introduce eagles to a wide audience – both in the flesh and on television. He appeared in commercials, natural history films, children's television and even in pop videos.

In 1984, I was asked to appear on *Wogan* and I took Sebastian with me. It was by far the most important interview I had ever been asked to give and it went out live too, so I was a little nervous. When I arrived at the Shepherd's Bush studios, I anxiously read the typed list of questions which, I was told, Terry Wogan was going to ask me. As it turned out, I needn't have bothered, because Terry, who I gathered was not at all keen on appearing with animals in general and with a golden eagle in particular, was so dumb struck by Sebastian that he totally ignored his autocue – clearly extremely nervous of Sebastian's proximity – and stuttered out the first questions which came into his head. Sebastian was unperturbed. He had seen the inside of many television studios before and he yawned and passed a dropping on the floor. Whilst attempting to answer the questions sensibly and trying not to laugh at Sebastian's antics, I was annoyed to see that the boom microphone, which is often held suspended over interviews, just out of shot, was being waved about above Sebastian's head. Hawks hate having anything moving about above them – they feel threatened by it. I had already stressed that our radio mikes should be used and not the boom, but clearly my request had not been taken seriously. I could feel through my glove that Sebastian had tensed and the next moment he bated, launching himself off the glove in the direction of Wogan. With my grip on his jesses (the leather straps fastened around his legs) I quickly had him back under control. I glared at the boom operator – the boom was hastily withdrawn and Sebastian relaxed again instantly, but Terry was shocked out of his wits. The audience, however, thought it was extremely funny and it brought the house down. The interview made the *Best of Wogan* that Christmas.

In 1993, I was asked by a production company to write and present a film on eagles for Kellogs, the breakfast cereal company. It was shot over three days and Sebastian was featured heavily. Throughout the first two days, he was his normal, sunny-natured self. In quiet moments, I posed with him for the stills photographer on the moor, sitting below him as he perched on the trunk of a tree. On the last morning of the shoot, we had a half-hour drive to another location at the edge of a loch. Sebastian – a seasoned traveller, both in the car and on aeroplanes – hopped into his special travelling crate and we set off. When we arrived at the location, I opened his box and to my horror, he staggered out and collapsed on the ground. Whilst I had to do my piece to camera with another eagle – one of the hardest things I have ever had to do in my life – Steve rushed Sebastian to the vet. He was dead on arrival. The post-mortem revealed apoplexy – a rupture of the brain artery. In tears, we buried him on the moor, under the tree where he had perched so happily just twenty-four hours earlier. As news of his death spread, we were inundated with phone calls and letters of tribute from former students, other falconers and media people who had worked with him. Ironically, one of my pieces to camera the day before had been on the subject of longevity in eagles. Large eagles, I had explained, like the golden eagle, could live in captivity for seventy or eighty years. Sebastian had been fourteen.

There is a brighter postscript to Sebastian's story. Shortly after his death, we were contacted by Edinburgh Zoo who offered us on permanent loan their female golden eagle, named Bennan. Bennan's parents had been shot on the Isle of Lewis twenty years previously and their orphaned eaglet had been taken to the zoo to be reared. Bennan had been there ever since. Many attempts had been made to pair her up for breeding. She had laid eggs and the zoo had attempted to artificially inseminate her. She had even reared a buzzard chick, but she had never bred herself. She was offered to us to see if, after twenty years of relative inactivity, we could get her flying.

To our delight and amazement we found that Bennan, like Sebastian, had an exceptionally sweet nature. We took her carefully through her training, as, not surprisingly, she was desperately unfit, but now she is flying free and catching rabbits. The name 'Bennan' is a Gaelic word meaning 'free-spirit'. After twenty years in a cage, Bennan's name is, perhaps, finally apt and we feel strongly that Sebastian's death inadvertently gave Bennan a new lease on life.

In 1991, Steve and I had begun to run into trouble. The major recession which had the whole country in its grip, was at its worst in the south-east of England. Our course bookings began to fall off, as interest rates soared. Like so many people, we had made the mistake of borrowing heavily in the boom years and for a while, everything we had touched had turned to gold. When the recession hit, we had to fight for our survival and acting on advice given to me by my father just before he died that autumn, we decided to act quickly, put our houses on the market and relocate. The question of where we would relocate to was never debated as the answer was obvious to both of us – Scotland. Only in Scotland, where the environment was so much better suited to flying our hawks and where the picturesque beauty of the hills seeped into the core of our beings, would we be able to get over the ripping apart of our business and the loss of our lovely house.

Acting swiftly, we put the houses on the market early in 1992, pulled up roots and went north, away from the rat-race in the south, away from the Channel Tunnel project (which was dissecting Kent with its road and rail links) to the area of central Perthshire which we had grown to know and to love since 1984.

Although at the time it seemed like a last-ditch effort to save our business, it turned out to be the best move we could have possibly made. We moved into a rented cottage on the Braco Castle Estate, three minutes below the grouse moor which we had rented annually since 1989. Eight miles down the road lies the world-famous Gleneagles Hotel. This 230-bedroomed hotel is justifiably renowned for the quality of its leisure facilities, including its excellent championship golf courses. Amongst its many attributes, Gleneagles includes the Jackie Stewart Shooting School and the Mark Phillips Equestrian Centre. In the winters of 1989 and 1990, Steve and I had run week-long falconry courses at Gleneagles for their guests. When Gleneagles heard that the British School of Falconry was now moving right on to their doorstep, they contacted us and invited us to open a branch of the school there, on their 830-acre estate.

The British School of Falconry is now running successfully at Gleneagles and a wealth of opportunities have come our way since the cementing of this happy liaison. A chance encounter with a guest at the hotel, Philip Tose, resulted in his multi-national financial services company, Peregrine, sponsoring an advanced new complex to house our hawks. Peregrine then sponsored a lavish and beautifully produced book which I wrote, called simply *Peregrine*, which was published in 1993. To my pride and delight, this book was described in a book review by *The Times* newspaper as 'one of the most beautiful bird books you are likely to see'.

My year is now focused around the changing seasons, which colour the life cycle of our hawks and the hawking seasons themselves. For me, the year starts in February, when the previous season's hawking draws to a close. The weather at this time of year is frequently bitterly cold and snowy. The first February we spent in

Scotland, we had snow up to our windowsills and drifts higher than the Range Rover. Even the simplest tasks of feeding and caring for the hawks were rendered extremely difficult. Floods and gales followed and lying in bed one night under the eves of our cottage, listening to the ferocity of the wind outside, we made the decision to move to a bedroom downstairs. No sooner had we settled again than we heard a ripping sound, followed by a crash and the wooden roof apex directly over where we had been sleeping snapped in two like a matchstick. We learned quickly never to make any elaborate plans for February, as we are frequently snowed in for days at a stretch.

In March, if the weather improves, our peregrines start their courtship displays. Having bred many different species of hawks over the years, we now breed only peregrines and the resulting progeny ensure that we can supply ourselves with high-flying grouse hawks. I fumigate, scrub and set up our table-top incubators in readiness to receive the precious eggs.

The first eggs are laid in April. The pairs are left to incubate them for the first week, then they are collected carefully and brought indoors to the incubators. Two weeks later, the pairs recycle and lay a second clutch, which is left with them. Having a clutch of valuable eggs in an incubator is rather like playing God. Looking at the incubators, it is hard to believe that these mechanical boxes of tricks can successfully emulate a falcon and I worry about them constantly. Incorrect humidity, fluctuations in temperature and many other problems can result in the loss of an embryo or indeed of a whole clutch. The more I worry, the more equipment I buy – power-cut alarms, an invertor which cuts in if the mains electricity cuts out, special precision scales to monitor the weight of the egg to the nearest tenth of a gram on a daily basis – all this paraphernalia goes into ensuring that each baby peregrine enjoys the best possible chances of survival.

When the first chick hatches in May, I welcome it out of the egg with great enthusiasm. By the time the last youngster is returned to its parents to be reared in late June, after countless hours of feeding chicks and clearing up after chicks, I am relieved to see the back of it.

I don't want to see the chicks again until they have grown a full set of feathers and are ready to start their training.

Throughout the summer, I run the office, assist our two instructors at Gleneagles with the teaching, attend endless meetings and escape into the peace of the surrounding countryside with a hawk for some summer rabbit hawking whenever I can. Periodically I fly down to London to attend a meeting in my capacity as an elected member of the 'Hawk Board' – the government advisory panel on captive hawks. My mother and stepfather live in East Sussex and Charlie is now the manager of a model shop in London, so sadly I don't see them as often as I would like, but whenever I have an excuse to go south, I try to visit them. In the summer months our adult peregrines are moulting, so we leave them loose in aviaries for as long as possible, taking them out just in time to get them going for the opening of the grouse season.

The young peregrines are taken up for training first, usually during the last week of July. I select my eyass – as a hawk taken from the nest is correctly termed – fit her 'furniture', or equipment, and begin her training. She should be ready to fly free from the creance – the light line on which she is initially called to the lure – about ten days later. The adults come out of the aviaries in early August. They will remember their training, but they will be grossly unfit – as indeed will we when we first start walking on the moor. From 12 August to the close of the season on 10 December, we will attempt not to miss a single day of sport and I will endeavour to fit in all my other work around the hawking.

At the start of the season, the weather can be hot and midgy and we will avoid going out until the cool of the evening. The dogs are unfit too, so the pace is slow but the exercise is still strenuous. In September, the sport improves as both the peregrines and the young grouse begin to fly more strongly. By October, dogs, hawks and falconers will be working as a team and providing the grouse play ball too, we will have some spectacular flights. We take no clients on the hill – our grouse hawking is purely for our own pleasure. Other falconers and friends will frequently stay with us through the season to watch and participate in this rare and enthralling branch of our sport. They need to be fit to keep up, as by October, Steve and I are Herculean from all the walking, with leg muscles which Arnold Schwarzenegger would be proud of.

In November, the weather tends to take a turn for the worse and by December we are often hawking in snow. Our outings begin to resemble an exercise in Arctic endurance. We don thermals and heavy Barbour jackets and fortify ourselves with a hip flask and the dogs with Mars bars. We vie to catch a grouse on 10 December and we finish the season with mixed feelings of regret and relief, as we head for the fireside to write up our game book and plan our campaign for the next season.

We work hard over Christmas and the New Year, as the school at Gleneagles is open every day of the year and during the festive season we are always busy with guests, who want to take a lesson or hunt rabbit, pheasant and duck with our Harris hawks. At the end of January, we tot up our annual hawking total and open a fresh page of the game book for the coming season.

Reflecting on my life to date, I am aware of how enormously fortunate I have been to be able to make a living out of the sport I love. I have been privileged to share my passion for falconry with others, through the school and through my books. Every day the phone is busy with calls from former students and enthusiasts, telling me about their hawks and about the pleasure that falconry has given them. Ebony is preening on the lawn outside – she is still catching rabbits at the age of twenty-four – and Steve and I are in the process of buying another beautiful country house nearby.

The sport of falconry and the hawks I use in the chase continue to fill my every waking moment and frequently my dreams too – just as they have from the first day I clapped eyes on a falcon. My life has been immeasurably enriched by raptors and for this I will be eternally grateful.